Heather Christo's
GENEROUS TABLE

Heather Christo's GENEROUS TABLE

EASY & ELEGANT RECIPES THROUGH THE SEASONS

PHOTOGRAPHY BY

Heather Christo & Jim Henkens

Kyle Books

For my mother Susan,
my first and best teacher.

Published in 2013 by Kyle Books
an imprint of Kyle Cathie Limited
www.kylebooks.com

Distributed by National Book Network
4501 Forbes Blvd., Suite 200
Lanham, MD 20706
Phone: (800) 462-6420
Fax: (301) 429-5746
custserv@nbnbooks.com

10 9 8 7 6 5 4 3 2 1

ISBN: 978-1-906868-90-1

Project editor Anja Schmidt
Art direction & design Lisa Berman
Food Photography Heather Christo
Lifestyle Photography Jim Henkens
Food styling Jean Galton & Anne Miska
Prop styling Heather Christo & Lisa Berman
Copy editor Sarah Scheffel
Production by Nic Jones, Gemma John & Lisa Pinnell

Library of Congress Control No. 2013930179

Color reproduction by Alta Image
Printed and bound in China by C&C Offset Printing Co., Ltd

Contents

Introduction

Even as a child, I loved to delight people with food. I spent my youngest years in the neighbor's potting shed turning mud pies into wedding cakes and trying to coerce every kid in the neighborhood into playing restaurant, with me as chef, of course. My brothers tromped in muddy from soccer practice on a school night, while I was wrapping up my daily chore of setting the table. They rolled their eyes as I put the finishing touches on my hand-printed place cards, the little bud vases of flowers collected from my mother's garden and the tall tapered candles in brass candlesticks that my mother allowed me to light carefully before dinner.

Bless her heart, my mother let me develop this love of food and presentation without waving me away (which would have been the easy thing to do on a busy night with four kids to feed). Instead, she showed me how to make the salad dressing and garnish the lasagna or roast chicken with fresh herbs, and how to properly fold the cloth napkins. She is a great hostess and, watching her, I saw the effects of sharing a wonderful meal. Good food and generosity never loses its ability to calm us, connect us, inspire and nourish us. So, it was in my mother's kitchen and around my childhood table that I first learned the alluring spirit that delicious, beautiful, homemade food could create. I was hooked.

After studying art in college, my love of food led me to Le Cordon Bleu in San Francisco, where I stayed on to work in French pastry. Back in Seattle, I catered and private-cheffed for years and found inspiration in the tremendous seasonal produce that was suddenly all around me, in the local farmers' markets, co-ops, and food stores. More and more, my cooking style came to be defined by delicious fresh ingredients, simply but perfectly prepared. And as a result, the recipes in this book make the most of my favorite seasonal fruit and vegetables.

From Cooking to Writing

But despite all of my environmental influences, the greatest inspiration by far is my family and our friends. My husband, Pete, very romantically (and quickly!) swept me off my feet and before I knew it, I was married, had two baby girls and hung up my chef togs for a family. With Pete's encouragement, I started a blog as a way to collect recipes, express a little creativity and stay organized in my world, which was getting more disorganized by the minute (if you have ever had a baby, you know what I mean!).

However babies grow and mature. And, as my little girls did just that, so did my blog. I started to add tips on entertaining, menus, flowers and drinks, and my readers loved it. My cooking style evolved, too, as a result of creating food that my family really *wants* to eat. Elevated comfort food made with the freshest ingredients possible, as well as a balance of flavors, textures, and color, such as an Asparagus Walnut Pesto Linguini in spring, Sweet and Spicy Pineapple Barbecued Chicken in summer, Pumpkin Gingersnap

Trifle in autumn, and Roasted Beef Tenderloin with Parsley Cream Sauce for the holidays in winter. And don't forget the beverages: In addition to hints on setting up bubbly or liquor-tasting bars, I also include fun cocktails like a Blackberry Jalapeño Margarita. Because we can all use a good drink at the end of a long day!

A Cookbook with Benefits

I am most concerned with making food that is not only beautiful to look at but tastes amazing; generous, bountiful food you find yourself thinking about days later, cooked from recipes that will last a lifetime. But I wanted to give you more than a cookbook. So, as I set out to write this "cookbook with benefits," the first place I went was to friends and my blog readers. After all, they are who I write for: Busy people with full-swing families or careers, often both, who are trying to "do it all," including being "domestic goddesses."

I asked them what their biggest challenge is in having people over for meals. Overwhelmingly, the response was: Knowing how to pull it all together. And so, as this is exactly what I have done professionally for years, and is now the way I live my life—with a constant stream of friends and family, food and drinks, parties big and small—I've shared lots of my tips and tricks for entertaining. In addition to my recipes, there are menus for every kind of get-together—Easter Feasts, Anniversary Parties, Backyard BBQs, Christmas Morning Breakfasts—and ideas for those simple but effective creative touches that are guaranteed to transform every meal into an easy and elegant occasion!

Celebrating Every Day

To create this book, I spent a year making notes on the wedding showers, baby showers, holiday celebrations, family birthdays and the many wonderful meals I shared with the people I love. When I write for my blog, I think of my posts as love letters to my two young daughters, a way to give them a detailed account of their childhood foods and celebrations. As I wrote this book, I thought of it as a love letter to each person who strives to create an environment that nourishes his or herself, family, and friends. Being a wife, a mother, a sister, a daughter, a friend, and a working woman is hard work. When anyone wants to cook or entertain for large groups, or even just for their own family, I want to help make it easy and enjoyable. So this book is for you, and it is about what I love to do: Sharing the love of food with friends and family.

HChristo

CHAPTER ONE

Spring

In the Pacific Northwest, I always know that spring is here by the arrival of the hummingbirds that nest in our back yard. They start buzzing about in early March, and it is a wonderful reminder for me to get going in the garden so that they will have plenty to eat. Another reminder comes in the form of the young green asparagus, chives and fiddlehead ferns that poke their heads through the cold, wet earth and make their way to my salad bowl. My little daughters delight in the bouquets they help me arrange from all of the purple and yellow spring bulbs that bloom in the front yard. I love spring and as every day grows lighter and warmer, I take joy in the produce that pops up, more prevalent every week, and in the fresh cooking inspiration that comes with a new season.

SPRING MENUS

Early Spring Dinner

There is no better feeling than when the fresh green buds and grass of spring start to chase away the gray of winter. I love to kick off spring with a grownup dinner party after months of being cooped up with the kids. I go heavy in the kitchen with the hearty late-winter bounty, like cauliflower and lemons, as spring is just emerging. And fresh asparagus is always a good sign that warmer days are just around the corner, so I like to include some as well.

This table was so fun for me, as I adore anything saturated in color. Bright green watercress, wheatgrass and moss, all inexpensive and easy to find at this time of year, became the centerpiece, and, despite their humble beginnings, look quite glamorous in a rustic way. I also used bright green linens and my odd assortment of green glass pieces that I've collected over the years. This look could be re-created in any color palette.

USING TABLE LINENS

A few great tablecloths and other table linens can make a tremendous difference in the visual appeal of a table. Over the last 10 years, I have collected some very basic white linens, predominantly from tag sales and vintage shops. I still use my grandmother's tablecloths from the 1940s on a regular basis.

Brightly colored linens make an instant and bold impact, however, they can be hard to find and very expensive. I go to a fabric store where I can choose the color and fabric myself. Truth be told—I am a terrible seamstress, so I just use hem tape when setting the table!

If your linens are silk, they'll need to be dry-cleaned. I prefer to launder cotton linens myself, using cold water and mild detergent; for stains I use a paste of equal parts white vinegar and baking soda. Always air-dry!

Cauliflower Soup

While my husband has a total aversion to vegetables for the most part, one of his exceptions (besides any salad drenched in blue cheese dressing) is cauliflower. Clearly I cannot explain this at all, but I roll with it as best I can! Since I am able to grow cauliflower in my garden most of the year, and because it is so easy to find the rest of the time, this soup has become a regular for our family. The creamy white color you get by using water instead of broth is just lovely. I highly recommend a tiny drizzle of truffle oil over the top if it is available.

SERVES 4 TO 6
PREP TIME: 10 MINUTES
COOK TIME: 30 MINUTES

2 tablespoons unsalted butter

½ yellow onion, roughly chopped

kosher salt

6 cups roughly chopped cauliflower stems and florets (2 small heads)

4 cups water

½ cup heavy cream

truffle oil, for garnish (optional)

1 In a large heavy pot, melt the butter over low heat. Add the onion and sprinkle with salt. Cook over low heat until the onions are soft and translucent, stirring frequently to ensure that they do not brown, 5 to 6 minutes.

2 Add the cauliflower to the pot and the water. Simmer, covered, over low heat for about 25 minutes.

3 Remove the pot from the heat and, working in batches, puree the soup in a blender on high speed until it is very smooth and creamy. Transfer back to a clean soup pot and stir in the cream. Season with salt.

4 Ladle into small bowls and garnish with a drizzle of truffle oil, if desired.

Asparagus Walnut Pesto Linguini

Every year those beautiful green crisp stalks of asparagus roll in, and every year I struggle with how to prepare them in new and delicious ways. In this spring pasta recipe, I combine them with toasted walnuts and Parmesan to create a pesto, which I toss with hot linguini.

SERVES 4 TO 6
PREP TIME: 10 MINUTES
COOK TIME: 12 MINUTES

8 ounces asparagus, trimmed and cut into 1-inch lengths

1 pound linguini

2 cloves garlic

⅓ cup toasted walnuts

¼ cup olive oil

¼ cup fresh lemon juice

½ cup finely grated Parmesan, plus more for garnish

kosher salt and freshly ground black pepper

1 First make the asparagus walnut pesto: Bring a large pot of salted water to a boil. Prepare a bowl of ice water. Place the asparagus in the boiling water and cook for 1 to 2 minutes, until bright green and tender-crisp. Transfer the asparagus to the ice bath to stop the cooking. Reserve the large pot of boiling salted water.

2 Add the linguini to the pot of boiling water. Cook to al dente, according to package directions. Drain and transfer to a serving bowl.

3 While the pasta is cooking, in the bowl of a food processor, combine the garlic and walnuts, asparagus, oil, and lemon juice. Pulse until a thick pesto has formed; it should still have some texture to it. Transfer to a bowl and fold in the Parmesan. Season with salt and set aside.

4 Toss the asparagus pesto with the hot pasta and serve with a generous sprinkle of Parmesan and black pepper to taste over the top.

Halibut en Papillote

There is a beautiful simplicity to cooking fish en papillote, which is the French phrase for "in parchment." I don't want to jinx myself, but I am pretty sure if you follow these instructions, you cannot mess this up: It will be flawless every single time. The parchment steams the fish in the butter, lemon, and thyme and it comes out moist and perfectly cooked—and isn't that the hardest part about preparing fish? This foolproof method makes this recipe so attractive for a dinner party. You can prepare everything earlier in the day and store your little parchment packages in the refrigerator. Then 15 minutes before you are ready to eat, pop them in the oven and voila! You get fresh brightly flavored, perfectly cooked halibut—and you look like a genius in the kitchen!

SERVES 4
PREP TIME: 10 MINUTES
COOK TIME: 15 MINUTES

4 tablespoons unsalted butter

4 large cloves garlic, minced

4 lemons

1 tablespoon fresh thyme leaves, plus 4 fresh thyme sprigs

four 4-ounce halibut fillets

kosher salt and freshly ground black pepper

1 Preheat the oven to 375°F and lay out four 8 x 8-inch circles of parchment paper.

2 In a small pan, melt the butter over low heat and add the garlic, the juice of two of the lemons, and the thyme. Continue to cook over low heat for 2 to 3 minutes, allowing the butter to absorb the flavors.

3 Slice the remaining 2 lemons into 6 round slices each. Place 3 lemon rounds on one half of each piece of parchment and top with a sprig of fresh thyme. Lay 1 halibut fillet on top of the lemons and thyme on each parchment circle. Sprinkle each fillet with salt and pepper.

4 Divide the butter sauce among the 4 fillets, pouring the sauce on top of the fish. Fold each parchment paper in half over the fillets, then pinch and fold over the edges to seal the packet. Place the packets on a sheet pan and bake for 12 minutes.

5 Remove the sheet pan from the oven and cut open the packets to release the steam. Serve the fish in the opened parchment papers.

Lemon Tart with an Almond Shortbread Crust

I am a sucker for lemon anything. But when it comes to lemon sweets, I obsess over lemon bars on a regular basis. To try something new, I thought I would spin them into an elegant lemon tart. And good thing I did because this is the best lemon tart I have ever made—or tasted, for that matter—and I can't help but share it with you. I love it with a pretty little scoop of Coconut Sorbet so that I can get all of my favorite goodies in one dessert. I hope you enjoy it as much as I do.

SERVES 8
PREP TIME: 15 MINUTES
COOK TIME: 30 MINUTES

ALMOND SHORTBREAD CRUST

2 cups all-purpose flour

1 cup powdered sugar, plus more for sifting

1 cup unsalted butter, cold

1 cup slivered almonds

½ teaspoon salt

handful of edible flowers, for garnish

LEMON FILLING

3 eggs

1½ cups granulated sugar

3 tablespoons all-purpose flour

zest of 3 lemons

½ cup fresh lemon juice

INGREDIENT NOTE:
Meyer lemons make for a nice substitution in this recipe as the flavor is more instense, reminding me of a lemon crossed with a grapefruit. They are easiest to find in the winter months.

1   Preheat the oven to 350°F. Prepare a 10-inch round tart pan with a removable bottom with cooking spray.

2   First make the almond shortbread crust: In the bowl of a food processor, combine the flour, powdered sugar, butter, almonds and salt. This crust has to have some sturdiness to it, so mix the dough until it has really come together and the almonds are completely combined. Transfer the dough to the prepared pan and, using your fingers or a spatula, firmly press the dough onto the bottom of the pan. Using your fingers, bring the dough up the sides of the tart pan to create a thick and even crust on the edges. Poke a few holes into the dough with a fork to release steam while par-baking the crust.

3   Bake for 15 minutes, until the crust is barely golden. When you take it out of the oven, press the crust down with a spatula to release any steam bubbles that may have formed. I also run a spoon along the inside sides of the pan to make sure there is a nice round edge on the sides of the crust.

4   While the crust is baking, make the lemon filling: In a medium mixing bowl, whisk the eggs until fluffy. Add the sugar, whisking constantly, until well combined. Add the flour and mix well. Finally whisk in the lemon zest and juice.

5   Pour the filling over the hot crust when it comes out of the oven, and return it to the oven to cook for another 15 minutes, until the custard is just set and a little golden on top. (Be careful that you don't add so much filling that it spills over the crust line—the custard will bake the crust to the pan, making it very difficult to remove.)

6   Let the tart cool in the pan for 15 minutes. While still warm, carefully pop the edge of the tart pan off the tart. Place the tart on a platter and cool completely.

7   When the tart is cool, sift powdered sugar over the top and garnish with the edible flowers. Slice the tart and serve each piece with a little freshly whipped, unsweetened whipped cream or a scoop of Coconut Sorbet (see page 21).

Coconut Sorbet

This is creamy, sweet and icy—a perfectly refreshing tropical dessert! To make sure that you can really taste the coconut flavor, I make this sorbet with a double hit of coconut (coconut milk and unsweetened dried coconut). This is an absolute favorite of my mother's—she likes to eat it solo—but it's also very good with the Lemon Tart, as shown, opposite.

GENEROUS TIP: You don't need an ice cream maker for this. You can simply freeze the sorbet in an airtight plastic container, see step 3.

MAKES 1 QUART
PREP TIME: 5 MINUTES
   PLUS FREEZING
COOK TIME: 5 MINUTES

2 cans coconut milk,
   well shaken

2 cups flaked
   unsweetened coconut

1 cup sugar

pinch of salt

1   In a medium pot, combine the coconut milk (make sure that you include all of the thick coconut cream stuck to the lid), flaked coconut, sugar and salt. Bring to a simmer over medium-low heat and stir for 2 to 3 minutes, or until the sugar has dissolved. Remove the pot from the heat and set aside to cool.

2   Once cooled, strain the coconut milk mixture through a fine-mesh sieve into a bowl, pressing all of the liquid out of the flaked coconut. Discard the flaked coconut; refrigerate the coconut milk mixture until cold.

3   Freeze the coconut sorbet in an ice cream maker, according to the manufacturer's directions, or alternatively place it in an airtight plastic container and freeze overnight. When ready to eat, scoop and serve immediately.

Greek Easter Feast

Until I met my husband, I had never really experienced Greek food, and certainly not authentic Greek food. While I have yet to go to Greece where he and his family are from, there is wonderful Greek food right in my own community. We are blessed to have a beautiful extended family and friends with whom Pete grew up. And there are some incredible cooks among this group, not least of all my mother-in-law, Tula.

Tula is amazing in the kitchen. She raised three boys with great appetites, so she knows a thing or two about feeding people! I think all of the years of cooking for a large family have left her with a very relaxed attitude in the kitchen and you can taste that in her food. Many of these dishes are recipes that she shared with me, not on recipe cards, but while working together in the kitchen. I observe her and make notes, practice techniques and occasionally add my own small twists on these delicious classic dishes.

This menu was created to honor Greek Easter, the most important of all Greek Orthodox occasions. While this meal would probably be considered a small spread for Greek Easter (ha!), it is a wonderful mix of dishes that are meant to be shared and passed around the table family style.

Dolmades

These tiny delicious bundles of seasoned rice wrapped in grape leaves are simmered in a very flavorful sauce until tender. I pile them, hot or cold, on a large platter and marvel as they rapidly disappear! They are just the right size for one bite, and when done well, will just fall apart in your mouth!

SERVES 8 TO 10
PREP TIME: 30 MINUTES
COOK TIME: 2 HOURS

one 15-ounce jar
   grape leaves

1¾ cups olive oil

2 cups minced
   green onions

2½ cups minced
   yellow onion

8 cloves garlic, minced

2 cups minced fresh
   flat-leaf parsley

½ cups loosely packed
   fresh dill

15 ounces tomato sauce

1½ cups white
   long grain rice

kosher salt and freshly
   ground black pepper

½ cup lemon juice

¼ cup water

1 Remove the grape leaves from the jar and gently rinse them under cool water. Place them in a large heavy pot and fill the pot with water to cover the leaves. Bring to a boil over medium-high heat. Once the water is boiling, set your timer for 7 minutes. Depending on the brand of grape leaves you use, they will either be done around this time or, if they are thick and dense, you will have to boil them for 15 minutes total. You will know that they are done when the leaves and stems are very tender and tear easily. Drain the water and rinse the leaves in cool water. Set aside.

2 In the same pot, heat ¾ cup of the olive oil over medium heat. Add the green and yellow onions and sweat until translucent about 10 minutes. Add the garlic, parsley and dill and cook another 2 minutes. Add the tomato sauce and rice. Stir well, then take the pot off of the heat. Season with salt and pepper. Let cool until you can easily handle the filling with your fingers.

3 When you are ready to assemble the dolmades, preheat the oven to 350°F.

4 Gently lay out 1 grape leaf and smooth it flat. Add 1 to 2 teaspoons of filling, depending on the size of the grape leaf, to the middle of the leaf. Tuck each of the sides over the filling, then pull the bottom over the filling and roll into a small log.

5 Repeat with the rest of the leaves and filling.

6 Arrange the dolmades snuggly in a 10-inch round baking dish in a concentric circle. It is okay to double stack them.

7 In a bowl, combine the remaining 1 cup olive oil, lemon juice and water, then pour it over the dolmades so that the liquid covers them. Place a 10-inch dinner plate on top of the dolmades to weigh them down. Liquid will come up around the plate. Place the baking pan in the oven, and bake for 1 hour and 30 minutes.

8 When you remove the pan from the oven, very carefully lift the dinner plate off of the dolmades. (Watch out for steam!) The dolmades should be very tender and the rice filling should be plump and moist.

9 Pile the dolmades onto a platter. They can be served, hot, warm or cold.

Spanikopita

Spanikopita reminds me of American potato salad in that everyone's mother makes it a little differently. Tula was raised in Athens and loves to flavor hers with a generous amount of leek, green onion and fresh dill. Other friends from more mountainous regions use mint. I'm sharing Tula's version here, which has crispy, buttery, delicate layers of filo dough and the perfect amount of creamy, salty filling sandwiched in the center. The egg-rich custard is filled with fresh spinach, herbs and onion and studded with gooey, melting feta and cottage cheese. These are best served hot, but I also love them cold the next day. These could even be served at brunch in place of quiche.

GENEROUS TIPS: The addition of cream of wheat is Tula's trick to keep the filling from getting the filo soggy. Be relaxed with the filo: Tula's technique for dealing with tears is to just overlap the layers in the opposite direction so that any tears are covered. You do not need additional salt in the filling, the feta should be salty enough.

SERVES 8 TO 10
PREP TIME: 20 MINUTES
COOK TIME: 60 MINUTES

2 medium leeks,
   finely sliced

2 bunches green onions,
   finely sliced

1 yellow onion, minced

5 cups spinach,
   rinsed well,
   dried and
   finely shredded

1 cup olive oil

8 large eggs

1 cup cottage cheese

1½ pounds feta

½ cup fresh dill

¼ cup cream of wheat

freshly ground
   black pepper

½ cup (1 stick) unsalted
   butter

1 pound filo dough

1 Preheat the oven to 350°F.

2 In a large bowl, toss the leeks, green and yellow onions and spinach with ⅓ cup of the olive oil.

3 Crack the eggs into a separate bowl and beat them until fluffy. Add the beaten eggs to the vegetable mixture, along with the cottage cheese, feta, and dill. Mix well with clean hands, making sure to separate the rings of leek and green onion and mixing in the cottage cheese and feta. Add a few pinches of freshly ground black pepper and the cream of wheat.

4 In a small pan, melt the butter and then stir in the remaining ⅔ cup olive oil.

5 Lay out the stack of filo dough flat on your work surface. Using a brush, butter a 13 x 18 x 1-inch rimmed sheet pan with the butter and oil mixture.

6 Peel a sheet of filo dough off the stack and lay it down the long way on the sheet pan. Follow with another good brush of the butter and oil.

7 For the next layer, arrange 2 sheets of filo on the pan the short way, overlapping in the middle and extending past the edges of the pan. Then brush with more butter and oil.

8 Add 3 more layers of filo, alternating between the long way and the short way and brushing with the butter and oil in between.

9 Spread the filling evenly over the top of the filo dough, then add 3 more layers of filo on top, the long way, with butter and oil brushed in between each layer. Fold any overhanging filo over the top and brush down with butter and oil. Lay one final sheet on top the long way, and brush generously with butter and oil.

10 Lightly slice the top of the spanikopita into 4-inch squares, and then firmly cut the squares into triangles. Bake for about an hour, until golden brown.

11 Slice the spanikopita into the pre-made triangles and serve immediately, or chill and serve cold.

Laganes Sesame Bread

Try talking to my husband, my mother-in-law or any of my other Greek friends and family about pita bread (and hummus, for that matter) and you will be shut down. Pita bread is not Greek. Apparently. And the feelings are quite, uh, strong about this. However, I still needed a good flatbread to hold my Lamb Meatballs (see page 31) and dip in all my favorite Greek dips (see page 29). Laganes was the answer. Laganes is a traditional Greek Lent bread made with just yeast, flour and water. I added a little sugar to help the yeast rise and some olive oil to make the bread more chewy and moist. Then I brushed a touch of egg white over the top and sprinkled with sesame seeds.

MAKES 8 ROUNDS
PREP TIME: 30 MINUTES
(plus 1 to 3 hours rising time)
COOK TIME: 10 MINUTES

two ¼-ounce packages
  active dry yeast

2 cups hot water
  (110 to 115°F)

2 tablespoons sugar

1 tablespoon kosher salt

4 tablespoons olive oil,
  plus more for greasing

5½ cups all-purpose flour,
  plus more for rolling

1 egg white, beaten

toasted sesame seeds,
  for garnish

1 In the bowl of a standing mixer fitted with a dough hook, combine the dry yeast, hot water and sugar. Let the yeast bloom for 10 to 15 minutes.

2 Add the salt, olive oil and half of the flour and mix on low speed to combine. Continue to mix in the rest of the flour, a little at a time. When all of the flour has been incoporated, mix over medium speed for 3 to 5 minutes, or until a nice smooth dough has formed.

3 Grease the inside of a large clean bowl with a little olive oil and place the dough in the bowl. Cover the bowl with plastic wrap and set somewhere warm to rise, at least an hour and up to 3 hours. The dough should be doubled in size and nice and puffy.

4 When you are ready to make the bread, preheat the oven to 425°F, and line two sheet pans with Silpat liners or parchment paper.

5 Turn the dough out onto a lightly floured countertop. Cut into 8 even pieces. Roll each piece out with a heavy rolling pin until it is about ¼ inch thick. (The dough is very elastic, and you should not have much trouble with sticking.) Place the rounds on the sheet pans (you may have to bake these in 2 batches if your 8 rounds don't fit on 2 sheets pans). Brush the tops lightly with the beaten egg white and sprinkle with sesame seeds.

6 Bake the bread for about 10 minutes, or still pale but slightly golden around the edges.

7 Serve hot or at room temperature.

Kopanisti Dip

This recipe was something I had to track down in a very roundabout way. After a friend requested it, I went through several of the Greek grandmothers in our community before someone finally called their sister in Greece to ask, "What goes in this dip?" After receiving a rough ingredient list, I just sort of winged it. So, this kopanisti may not be authentic, but I promise it is so delicious! I use it as a dip, a sandwich spread and as a body cream. (Just kidding about the body cream.)

MAKES 1½ CUPS
PREP TIME: 5 MINUTES

12 ounces feta cheese, drained and cubed

4 ounces roasted red peppers, drained

1 cup fresh mint leaves

¼ cup olive oil

3 small cloves garlic

2 tablespoons fresh lemon juice

¼ teaspoon red pepper flakes

1   In the bowl of a food processor, puree all of the ingredients together until smooth and well combined, but still with some texture.

2   Serve immediately or refrigerate for up to 5 days until ready to use.

Tzasiki

Again, I am struggling with being traditional. Or non-traditional, I suppose. Many love their tzasiki chunky and thick. I happen to like mine like a sauce that can be drizzled over my Lamb Meatballs (page 31) or even used as a salad dressing.

MAKES 2½ CUPS
PREP TIME: 10 MINUTES

1 cucumber

2 cups Greek yogurt

¼ cup roughly chopped onion

1 clove garlic

⅛ cup fresh dill

1 tablespoon fresh oregano

½ tablespoon olive oil

2 teaspoons white wine vinegar

kosher salt

1   Peel and grate the cucumber into a strainer. Let it sit while you combine the rest of the ingredients in the bowl of a food processor.

2   Squeeze the extra water out of the cucumber (you should have about ¾ cup cucumber), then add it to the food processor.

3   Pulse everything together until smooth and pour into a bowl. Season with salt to taste. Serve chilled.

4   Serve immediately or refrigerate for up to 3 days until ready to use.

Greek Village Salad

If you hear me lament about my husband's aversion to fresh vegetables, let me just shout loudly that this salad is a massive exception. Whether it is because he was raised on the stuff, because it is so fresh and delicious, or even just because it has the word "Greek" in the name, he will eat it by the boat load. Truly.

SERVES 8 TO 10
PREP TIME: 10 MINUTES

GREEK VINAIGRETTE

1 clove garlic, minced

3 tablespoons olive oil

3 tablespoons red
   wine vinegar

1 teaspoon dried oregano

kosher salt and freshly
   ground black pepper

4 cups roughly chopped
   ripe tomatoes (about
   1½ pounds)

3 cups peeled and roughly
   chopped cucumbers
   (about 2)

2 red or yellow peppers,
   cut into chunks

½ red onion, thinly sliced

½ cup pitted kalamata olives

8 ounces feta, drained

freshly ground black pepper

1 First make the Greek vinaigrette: In a small bowl, whisk together the garlic, olive oil, red wine vinegar and oregano until well combined. Season with salt and pepper. Set aside until ready to use.

2 In a large bowl, combine all of the vegetables and gently toss together. Pour the Greek vinaigrette over the vegetables, and again, gently toss to coat them. Crumble the feta over the salad and then very gently toss the cheese into the vegetables.

3 I like to add a few more twists of freshly ground black pepper over the top of the salad before serving. Serve immediately at room temperature or chill before serving.

Lamb Meatballs

These are a masterpiece as far as meatballs are concerned. The rich lamb is packed with the flavor of onion and fresh herbs, with just a touch of cooling mint. Unlike some meatball recipes that call for milk, these meatballs get additional moisture—and flavor—from bread soaked in red wine. While I typically bake or boil my meatballs, my mother-in-law Tula taught me the fantastic technique of pan-frying them. I love the crispy shell it gives them, especially with such a moist and juicy center.

SERVES 8 TO 10
PREP TIME: 20 MINUTES
COOK TIME: 10 MINUTES

quarter of a stale baguette

1 cup red wine

⅔ cup water

1¼ pounds ground lamb

¼ cup finely chopped green onion

1 cup minced yellow onion

4 cloves garlic, minced

½ cup finely chopped fresh mint

2 tablespoons finely chopped fresh oregano

½ cup finely chopped fresh flat-leaf parsley

2 large eggs, beaten

kosher salt and freshly ground black pepper

⅔ cup all-purpose flour

vegetable oil, for frying

olive oil, for frying

Laganes Sesame Bread (page 27)

Tzasiki (page 29)

1   In a medium bowl, tear the baguette into pieces (you should have about 2 cups). Cover the bread with the wine and water.

2   In a large bowl, combine the lamb, green and yellow onions, garlic, mint, oregano, parsley and eggs. Gently mix everything together with clean hands until well combined.

3   Partially squeeze the soaking liquid out of the baguette (reserving 1 to 2 tablespoons liquid), then gently break the bread up into the ground lamb mixture and stir it in. Add the reserved liquid and mix well. You will have a wet meat mixture.

4   In a small pan, fry up a small piece of the meat mixture. When it is cooked through, taste it for seasoning, and add salt and pepper if necessary.

5   Roll the meat mixture into 2-inch balls. (You will have about 30 meatlballs.) Place the flour in a shallow dish and lightly dredge each meatball in the flour, removing any excess. Set the meatballs aside on a sheet pan until they are all prepared.

6   In a large, deep sauté pan, add a combination of one-half vegetable oil and one-half olive oil until the oil is about ¼ inch deep. Heat the oil over medium heat. When the oil is hot, add the meatballs to the pan, filling the pan in a single layer (you might need to fry them in batches). Cook until the meatballs are brown and cooked through, turning them often, about 10 minutes. Keep them warm in a 325°F oven on a sheet pan.

7   Serve the meatballs hot or at room temperature, or freeze them for up to 4 months. To reheat them, bake them on a sheet pan at 350°F for 20 minutes. Serve them with the laganes sesame bread and tzasiki.

Bougatsa

I call this the lesser-known cousin of the very popular baklava. This is my husband's favorite dessert. Pete loves it for the rich and creamy custard that is enclosed in a blanket of crispy and buttery filo— with two layers of sweet and crunchy walnuts and cinnamon in between. (It's like of a crème brûlée stuffed in pastry!)

SERVES 12
PREP TIME: 15 MINUTES
COOK TIME: 50 MINUTES

1½ cups (3 sticks) unsalted butter

3 cups walnuts

1½ cups sugar

1 teaspoon cinnamon

7 large eggs

½ teaspoon kosher salt

2 teaspoons vanilla extract

8 ounces frozen filo dough, thawed

1   Preheat the oven to 350°F.

2   Melt the butter in a large saucepan over medium-low heat. Once it has melted, skim the foam off the top and discard. Reserve the remaining clear butter, which is called clarified butter.

3   In the bowl of a food processor, pulse the walnuts until they form coarse crumbs. Transfer to a medium bowl and stir in ½ cup sugar and the cinnamon.

4   In the same food processor bowl, combine the eggs, remaining 1 cup sugar, salt and vanilla and process until smooth and fluffy. Set the custard aside.

5   Brush a 9x13x3-inch deep baking dish with some of the clarified butter and then add one sheet of filo dough, gently pressing the dough into the pan (the edges of the dough will extend above the sides of the pan). Brush the filo dough with more clarified butter, and then add another layer (switching the direction of the filo dough). Add a third layer (again switching the direction of the dough).

6   Brush the top layer of filo with clarified butter and then sprinkle half of the walnut-sugar mixture on top, evenly distributing it. Add one more sheet of filo and brush with butter.

7   Pour the custard over, gently and evenly spreading it with a spatula. Lay a piece of filo on top and gently brush it with butter. Repeat.

8   Gently spread the remaining nut and sugar mixture over the filo dough. Add another three layers of filo and butter on top, alternating the direction of the layers. Fold all of the overhanging filo over the top of the pastry and generously brush the whole thing with the rest of the clarified butter.

9   Carefully score the top of the pastry into twelve 3-inch squares so that the filo won't puff up or shatter after baking. Bake for about 45 minutes, or until the filo is golden.

10   Let the bougatsa cool until the custard sets, about 30 minutes. Cut into squares along the scored lines and serve immediately.

Ladies' Luncheon

MENU

- FRESH ARTICHOKE SOUP

- HERB AND FLOWER SALAD
  WITH HONEY MUSTARD
  POPPY SEED DRESSING

- LEEK, HAM AND
  GRUYÈRE QUICHE

- BERRY FIZZ

- ALMOND RICOTTA POUND CAKE

- STRAWBERRY RHUBARB
  COMPOTE

My grandmother, Eleanor Jewett, better known as "Grammy" to all of her many grandchildren and great grandchildren, loved to entertain. When my dad was growing up, he said she and Grampy averaged two dinner parties a week. Can you imagine? I've seen the pictures and heard the stories to prove it—they were on fire! Even after she downsized to a condo for just herself, she was still throwing luncheons into her early nineties. She would get out the nice linens, china and crystal glasses and make sure that there was a pretty bunch of flowers on the table. Then she would whip up a quiche. Her lunches were always simple and elegant, with an emphasis on catching up with friends or grandchildren. That is what I've attempted to recreate here: a pretty, feminine luncheon that is light but still filling. This menu is just the thing for a birthday party or a small wedding or baby shower.

THE POWER OF A
GREAT HERB GARDEN

Here is the thing about herb gardens:
They take up very little space (my
own is made up of two little plots,
about 2 x 3 feet each) and the plants
produce nonstop for up to 9 months
out of the year. Choose herbs that
grow hearty in your region and you
will have an abundance of fresh
herbs for much of the year, and you
can dry your own herbs for the winter
months. (I sun-dry bay leaf, oregano
and thyme every year.) Here, in the
Northwest, I grow insane quantities
of chives, mint, oregano, sage, thyme
and edible flowers. I also squeak
out decent amounts of cilantro,
basil and parsley, even though I am
sure that they would prefer more
sun. These herbs provide me with
endless inspiration, and keep my food
tasting garden-fresh for pennies. And
because the herbs are perennials;
they come back year after year!

Fresh Artichoke Soup

In my search to make a soup that is not only brilliant green in color, but also brilliant in spring flavor, I ultimately found myself face to face with my favorite vegetable: the artichoke. It snuck in at the last moment and transformed my green soup into not only a thing of beauty, but into a "lick the bowl clean" kind of deliciousness. It is wonderful topped with a dollop of crème fraîche and some freshly snipped chives, or sprinkle a few Garlicky Croutons on top, a nod to that Mediterranean classic, stuffed, baked whole artichokes.

SERVES 4 TO 6
PREP TIME: 10 MINUTES
COOK TIME: 35 MINUTES

4 fresh artichokes

1 lemon, halved

3 tablespoons butter, plus more for buttering bread

1 yellow onion, peeled and large diced

kosher salt

4 cups fresh baby spinach leaves

1 quart water

½ cup heavy cream

1 slice of rustic bread

Crème fraîche, freshly snipped chives or Garlicky Croutons (page 162), for garnish

INGREDIENT NOTE: This is one recipe where it is really worth it to use fresh artichoke hearts: The flavor is unparalleled. However, if artichokes are not in season, be sure to use frozen artichoke hearts over canned—and never use artichokes packed in oil for this recipe.

1 Cut off and discard the stems from each artichoke. Cut off the top half of each artichoke. Pull or cut off all of the leaves until you get to the purple-tipped center leaves. Remove and discard those until you get to the hairy, spiky choke of each artichoke. You should have about 1½ cups of artichoke hearts.

2 Place the artichoke hearts and lemon halves in a small saucepan of salted water and lightly simmer over low heat, covered, for about 20 minutes. When the artichokes hearts are tender, remove from the water. Spoon the artichoke hearts out of the hairy chokes and slice the hearts into quarters. Set aside.

3 In a medium pan, melt the butter and add the onion with a sprinkle of kosher salt. Gently sweat the onion over low heat until very soft and tender, about 6 minutes. (You don't want the onions to brown so add a few tablespoons of water if the pan gets dry.) Set aside to cool slightly.

4 In a blender, combine the artichokes, spinach, and onion mixture with the water. Blend on high speed until the soup is completely smooth and a very bright green color.

5 Return the soup to a clean pot, and gently whisk in the cream. Season with salt and simmer the soup over medium heat for about 5 minutes, until hot but not boiling.

6 Ladle into bowls and top each serving with a dollop of crème fraîche and a sprinkle of chives or a few garlicky croutons. Serve immediately.

Herb and Flower Salad with Honey Mustard Poppy Seed Dressing

The addition of edible flowers adds color and soft texture to this simple and tender salad. I chose a dressing that is light enough not to overwhelm the baby lettuces and delicate blossoms, with enough flavor and natural sweetness to stand up to the fresh herbs. The result is so pretty and inherently feminine. You'll be left with half the dressing, so by all means, keep it in the fridge for up to one week for another use.

GENEROUS TIP: Anyone who has a flower garden or herb garden probably grows edible blossoms whether they know it or not. But if you're not sure if they're edible, look it up. Be sure to wash blossoms well, especially if you use fertilizer or pesticides.

SERVES 4 TO 6
PREP TIME: 10 MINUTES

HONEY MUSTARD POPPY SEED
 DRESSING

1 tablespoon chopped shallot

1 teaspoon Dijon mustard

1 tablespoon honey

¼ cup white wine vinegar

½ cup olive oil

kosher salt

1 teaspoon poppy seeds

8 cups mixed baby lettuces
 and herbs (such as fresh
 parsley and oregano
 leaves, dill or fennel fronds
 and torn sage, mint or
 thyme leaves)

1 cup assorted edible flowers
 (such as nasturtiums,
 rose petals, pansies,
 bachelor buttons and
 chive blossoms)

kosher salt and freshly
 ground black pepper

1   First make the dressing: In a blender, puree the shallot with the mustard, honey, vinegar, and olive oil until you reach a smooth consistency. Season with salt and gently stir in the poppy seeds.

2   In a large bowl, very gently toss the mixed greens and herbs with the dressing until the leaves are lightly and evenly coated. Sprinkle half of the edible flowers into the salad and gently toss.

3   Season with salt and pepper and garnish with the remaining edible flowers. Serve immediately.

Leek, Ham and Gruyère Quiche

I included this quiche in honor of my grammy, Eleanor. She just loved quiche, and I am not sure I ever remember one of her luncheons where she didn't make one. They are so easy and versatile once you get the hang of them (just like my baked eggs on page 155). You simply adjust the vegetables, protein, and cheese to suit the season or the event. For this one, I created a play on Grammy's favorite ham and green onion quiche, using smoked ham steak and sweet leeks. I also add a generous portion of Gruyère cheese, because, you know, the eggs and cream weren't going to make it rich enough. The result is fantastic and well suited to a breakfast, brunch or luncheon. I love it best served with a light salad on the side.

GENEROUS TIP: If the crust on the quiche starts to get too brown, loosely tent a piece of foil over the quiche and continue baking. Smoked ham steak is usually found next to the bacon in your supermarket.

MAKE AHEAD: For a head start, make the quiche crust the day before your luncheon.

SERVES 6 TO 8
PREP TIME: 20 MINUTES
  (plus 1 hour refrigeration time)
COOK TIME: 1 HOUR 15 MINUTES

QUICHE CRUST

2 cups all-purpose flour,
  plus more for rolling
  out the dough

½ teaspoon salt

¾ cup (1½ sticks) cold
  unsalted butter, cut into
  small pieces

1 large egg, beaten

2 tablespoons ice water

FILLING

2 tablespoons unsalted
  butter

1½ cups thinly sliced leeks

1 cup diced smoked
  ham steak

½ cup grated Gruyère cheese

8 large eggs

1 cup heavy cream

½ teaspoon kosher salt

pinch of nutmeg

freshly ground black pepper

1 First make the crust: In the bowl of a food processor, combine the flour, salt and butter. Pulse to a coarse crumb. Add the egg and pulse for a few seconds more. While still pulsing, dribble in the ice water until a sticky dough forms.

2 Turn the dough out onto a sheet of wax paper, and form it into a disc. Wrap the dough in the wax paper and refrigerate for at least 1 hour, or overnight.

3 Preheat the oven to 400°F, and prepare a 9-inch pie dish with cooking spray.

4 Turn the chilled dough out onto a lightly floured surface and, using a floured rolling pin, roll the dough out until it stretches over the 9-inch pie plate, leaving enough dough for a thicker crust around the edges. Use a fork to poke several sets of holes in the bottom of the pie dough (so that the crust doesn't puff up during par-baking). Place the pie plate on a sheet pan and bake for 20 minutes.

5 Meanwhile, make the filling: In a medium sauté pan, melt the butter over medium-low heat. Add the leeks and gently cook them until soft, 5 to 6 minutes (try not to let them brown.)

6 In a large bowl, whisk together the eggs, cream, salt, nutmeg and a few pinches of pepper until fluffy and well combined.

7 When the crust is done par-baking, leave it on the sheet pan and reduce the oven temperature to 350°F. Evenly layer the leeks, the diced smoked ham and the Gruyère on the bottom of the crust. Pour the egg mixture on top and bake the quiche for 50 minutes, until the crust is golden and the eggs have completely set.

8 Let the quiche cool for 5 to 10 minutes before slicing into it. Serve hot or at room temperature.

Berry Fizz

I always think of this drink as "nature's Italian soda." Instead of using a flavored syrup, I use fresh berries, mint and a touch of powdered sugar to flavor a big bubbling glass of cold club soda. The result is very refreshing and just a little sweet. A perfect drink for kids and adults alike!

SERVES 1
PREP TIME: 5 MINUTES

¼ cup fresh berries
    (such as raspberries
    and blackberries)

1 tablespoon fresh mint
    leaves, torn

1 teaspoon powdered sugar

ice cubes

6 ounces club soda, chilled

1   In the bottom of a tall glass, place the berries, mint leaves and sugar. Muddle the ingredients with a cocktail muddler or fork to create a pulp.

2   Fill the glass with ice cubes and top with the club soda.

3   Stir to combine and serve with a straw.

Almond Ricotta Pound Cake

This pound cake has gone through many incarnations, using all sorts of nuts and extracts. But my husband and older daughter, Pia, always chose the original almond as their favorite. My recipe was inspired by a yellow ricotta cake that a dear friend of mine makes from her Italian family's secret recipe. It is the staple yellow cake at every one of their family functions, and I am always first in line for a big chunk of it! If there is extra, I am back in line two minutes later. But seeing as how it is a secret recipe, I created my own rendition, which is becoming a bit of a staple in this family. I love this served with fresh or roasted fruit and whipped cream.

SERVES 8
PREP TIME: 10 MINUTES
COOK TIME: 1 HOUR

½ cup slivered almonds

¾ cup (1½ sticks) unsalted butter

1 cup ricotta cheese

1½ cups sugar

2 teaspoons almond extract

3 large eggs

1½ cups all-purpose flour

1 teaspoon baking soda

½ teaspoon salt

Strawberry Rhubarb Compote (opposite), for garnish

1   Preheat the oven to 325°F. Prepare a 9x5-inch loaf pan with baking spray.

2   Put the almonds in the bowl of a food processor and pulse until ground to a coarse flour. Set aside.

3   In the bowl of a standing mixer, cream the butter, ricotta and sugar until fluffy. Add the almond extract and the eggs and mix until well combined, scraping the sides of the bowl with a rubber spatula if needed.

4   In a separate bowl, combine the flour, ground almonds, baking soda and salt. Add the dry ingredients to the mixer and beat until well combined.

5   Pour the batter into the loaf pan and bake the cake for 1 hour 15 minutes, or until the top is golden and the center is set. (After about 30 minutes, start checking the cake; if it starts to get too brown, tent it with foil to finish baking.)

6   Remove the cake from the oven and let it cool on a rack until you can comfortably turn the cake out onto a platter or cutting board.

7   Slice the cake and serve warm or at room temperature with Strawberry Rhubarb Compote.

Strawberry Rhubarb Compote

This compote celebrates a winning duo, strawberry and rhubarb, in their most simple forms. The addition of just a bit of butter and sugar creates a beautiful pink sauce to pour over pound cake or a scoop of vanilla ice cream. I also enjoy stirring a heaping spoonful into a pitcher of lemonade.

MAKE AHEAD: You could make this up to 3 days ahead and bring up to room temperature or gently heat up before serving.

MAKES 3 CUPS
PREP TIME: 5 MINUTES
COOK TIME: 20 MINUTES

2 tablespoons unsalted butter

1 cup rhubarb, sliced into ½-inch pieces

2 cups strawberries, thinly sliced

½ cup sugar

In a large saucepan, melt the butter over medium-low heat. Add the rhubarb and strawberries, then cover with the sugar. Reduce the heat to low and simmer, stirring often, until the fruit is very soft and all of the sugar has dissolved, about 15 minutes. Serve hot or at room temperature, or keep in an airtight container in the fridge for 3 days.

Anniversary Party

MENU

- RHUBARB COOLER

- CUCUMBER CHILE MIGNONETTE

- BEET PESTO PASTA

- CRISPY POLENTA CUPS
  WITH CRÈME FRAÎCHE
  AND CAVIAR

- SEARED SEA SCALLOPS
  WITH ARTICHOKE PESTO

- ZUCCHINI LEMON CUPCAKES

Every year spring bursts with wedding anniversaries of those I love. Pete and I were married in May, as were my parents, my younger brother and several close friends. It's kind of a nonstop celebratory month, especially as time goes by and we commemorate more and more milestones. With this party, I honored my parents' 35th wedding anniversary, traditionally known as the coral anniversary. I not only played on coral in terms of color, but also in the menu. Every dish is kept light and seafood- or vegetarian-based.

I did a buffet for this party, so guests could gather and share in the spread. It was also a way to make very elegant food feel approachable and communal. The centerpiece is a multi-tiered serving platter filled with crushed ice and a gorgeous array of shellfish. I used old silver and silver-plated pieces that I dug out of my mother's and aunts' cupboards, as well as some of my own pieces that I have foraged from tag sales and thrift shops over the years.

The coral anniversary theme was especially fitting, as my parents have been avid collectors of coral and shells throughout their marriage, an obsession that must run in the family (wink, wink). I used pieces of that collection as part of the décor for the party. Since each shell or chunk of coral has a story attached, they were a walk down memory lane.

DETAILS TO BRING A THEME TOGETHER

You would be amazed at what small details can do to bring together the theme of an event. In this case, I added coral-colored stir sticks and paper straws to the drinks, and thematic cocktail napkins and labels for the food, giving the guests the impression that every little thing has been thought of—when, in fact, these items are small, inexpensive and easy to acquire or make. You can go so far as to create a signature cocktail, which not only keeps the theme flowing, but makes managing the bar easy for you as the host. And, keep in mind, it doesn't have to be a literal theme (like coral), even simply repeating a color in the ways I suggested above has a similar impact. A little can go a long way!

MAKING FLAVORED SIMPLE SYRUPS

Simple syrups are an amazing way to add complexity and sweetness to a drink. Think of simple syrup as a blank slate to create whatever flavor profile you want. You simply bring equal parts water and sugar to a boil (like 1 cup sugar to 1 cup water) and add whatever ingredient you want to infuse the syrup with. Some of my favorites include: mint, basil, fresh ginger, lemon juice, rhubarb, or blood orange juice. The truth is, you could really add just about any flavoring. Simmer the mixture for a few minutes and then you have the choice of pureeing or straining (I recommend both). Keep simple syrup in a jar in the refrigerator for up to two weeks. Use in cocktails like the Rhubarb Cooler on page 46, lemonades like the Cherry Mint Lemonade on page 77 or mix with chilled club soda for a refreshing spritzer.

Rhubarb Cooler

My mother has been growing rhubarb in her garden for as long as I can remember. Big bright red stalks full of sour pink flavor! I love rhubarb. And not just as a backup for strawberries. It is wonderful all on its own, especially if you enjoy sour with your sweet. I plucked a few stalks from my mother's garden and tried to think of how I could best incorporate the rhubarb into a special drink for her. A simple syrup brimming with rhubarb flavor and the most spectacular color was born. While I concocted this Rhubarb Cooler with a hint of sour lemon, spicy ginger, and vodka, you can add the rhubarb simple syrup to all types of cocktails, or even just club soda for a beautiful rhubarb spritzer.

MAKES 1 COCKTAIL
PREP TIME: 5 MINUTES
COOK TIME: 10 MINUTES

RHUBARB SIMPLE SYRUP

MAKES 1¼ CUPS

3 large stalks rhubarb,
    cut into 1-inch pieces

1 cup sugar

1 cup water

ice cubes

3 tablespoons Rhubarb
    Simple Syrup

1½ ounces vodka, chilled

1 lemon wedge

one ¼-inch-thick slice of
    fresh ginger

club soda, chilled

1 First make the simple syrup: In a medium saucepan over medium heat, combine the rhubarb, sugar and water and bring to a simmer. Reduce the heat to low and simmer, stirring occasionally, for about 10 minutes.

2 Strain the rhubarb mixture through a fine-mesh sieve into a bowl, making sure that you press all of the juice out of the rhubarb with the back of a spoon. Let cool before storing in an airtight container in the refrigerator up to 2 weeks.

3 To make the cocktail, fill a cocktail shaker with ice. Add the simple syrup, vodka, lemon wedge and ginger slice. Shake thoroughly then strain into a highball glass filled with ice. Top with the chilled club soda, stir and serve with a straw.

Cucumber Chile Mignonette

My first restaurant job consisted of, among other things, shucking oysters (uh, not easy!). It took me a while to really appreciate their beauty. At that point, I had never even contemplated eating an oyster. I remember trying to make the poor little gray lumps look as appealing as I could on a plate of shaved ice. As hard as that summer wrestling oyster shells was, I learned two very valuable things: One, how to shuck an oyster well (important life lesson, right?), and two, that I actually love eating them. Raw. My husband and I can literally take down dozens in an evening. In my opinion, that is best done with a liberal dose of mignonette. I like to add a bit more texture and flavor to the traditional vinegar and shallot version. Refreshing, crunchy cucumbers and spicy red chile lead the way to my more elaborate take on this classic shellfish accompaniment.

MAKES 1½ CUPS
PREP TIME: 5 MINUTES

1 cup peeled, seeded and diced cucumber

2 tablespoons minced shallot

1 tablespoon minced red chile pepper

½ cup red wine vinegar

Combine the cucumber, shallot, chile pepper and vinegar in a bowl. Serve chilled alongside raw oysters, clams and mussels.

Beet Pesto Pasta

If you haven't noticed yet, I have a bit of an obsession with pesto, which in my world means throwing something into a food processor with some other ingredients and creating a thick spread that I call pesto. But that's my problem. And, thank goodness it is, because it prompted me to throw beets in the food processor and make beet pesto, which, besides being absolutely extraordinarily tasty, is mind bogglingly beautiful. I serve this gorgeous pasta with pork or alongside a nice white fish—but it is also hearty enough to serve on its own as a vegetarian meal. I have also started serving small portions as appetizers at cocktail parties because I truly cannot get enough of this unique and eye-popping dish. Better still, my kids will eat entire bowlfuls without batting their pretty little eyes because, obviously, it's pink.

SERVES 4 TO 6
OR 24 AS AN APPETIZER
PREP TIME: 10 MINUTES
COOK TIME: 30 MINUTES

3 large purple beets, tops trimmed

3 cloves garlic

½ cup whole raw pistachio nuts, plus 2 tablespoons chopped, for garnish

¼ cup lemon juice

¼ cup olive oil

1 cup finely grated Parmesan

kosher salt

1 pound spaghetti

1 Bring a medium pot of salted water to a boil and add the beets. Boil until fork tender, 15 to 20 minutes.

2 Drain and rinse the beets with cold water and, using your fingers, rub the skin off the beets. Chop the beets into quarters and place them in the bowl of a food processor. Add the garlic, pistachios, lemon juice and olive oil and pulse until you have a smooth bright pink spread.

3 Using a spatula, fold in the Parmesan and season with salt. Set aside.

4 Bring a large pot of salted water to a boil and cook the spaghetti to al dente, according to package directions.

5 Rinse the spaghetti with cool water and drain well. Toss the spaghetti with the pesto and serve immediately. Garnish with extra Parmesan and the chopped pistachios.

Crispy Polenta Cups
with Crème Fraiche and Caviar

These little cups of crispy perfection have long been a special-occasion delight in my family. I love how the cups can be assembled days ahead of time, and then baked in the oven until golden and crispy after your guests have arrived. I always have the crème fraîche waiting in the refrigerator along with some freshly snipped chives. I simply pipe the filling and top with caviar and chives. Those that don't get popped directly into my mouth go onto the serving platter. The result is a crispy hot shell, with a cool, meltingly creamy center and a burst of salty, nutty caviar. The hint of mild onion flavor from the chives rounds out the experience. These are truly unforgettable.

GENEROUS TIPS: There are many varieties of caviar, and not all of them will break the bank. I personally love paddlefish, salmon roe, and varieties of tobiko, which are all very reasonably priced and widely available. Be sure to use a plastic or mother-of-pearl spoon for scooping to avoid tainting the caviar with a metallic flavor.

Wear long sleeves while stirring the polenta. It pops and spits at you while boiling, and trust me, you do not want a polenta burn.

It's easiest to pipe the crème fraiche if you use a piping bag. Since I am rarely organized enough to have one ready, I find that ketchup squeeze bottles work well, as do plastic resealable bags with the corner snipped off. If you do not have crème fraiche available, sour cream is a great substitute.

MAKES 24, SERVES 8
PREP TIME: 10 MINUTES
    (plus 1 hour refrigeration time)
COOK TIME: 40 MINUTES

1 quart chicken stock

½ teaspoon kosher salt

1 cup polenta

½ cup finely grated
    Parmesan cheese

1 tablespoon unsalted
    butter

kosher salt and freshly
    ground black pepper

¼ cup crème fraîche

2 ounces caviar

freshly snipped chives,
    for garnish

1   Prepare a 9 x 13 x 1-inch sheet pan with a little cooking spray.

2   In a large heavy saucepan, bring the chicken stock and salt to a boil over high heat. Reduce the heat to medium and whisk in the polenta, making sure there are no lumps. Use a wooden spoon to stir constantly for 15 to 20 minutes. (Yes, this will be a good workout.) When the polenta is ready, it will be thick and pull away from the sides of the pan.

3   Add the Parmesan and butter and stir until creamy. Remove the polenta from the heat and season with salt and pepper.

4   Pour the hot polenta into the prepared sheet pan and spread it smoothly until it is about 1 inch thick. Cover with plastic wrap and refrigerate for at least 1 hour or up to 2 days.

5   Using a cookie cutter or small glass, cut the polenta into 2-inch rounds. Arrange them on a clean sheet pan. Using a very small melon baller (although a small sharp paring knife would work, too), carefully hollow out the center of each polenta cup. Refrigerate, covered with plastic wrap, for another day, if you like.

6   When you are ready to bake, preheat the oven to 400°F.

7   Bake the polenta cups for 10 to 12 minutes, until golden and crispy.

8   Pipe or spoon the crème fraîche into the cups and immediately top each with ½ teaspoon of caviar. Garnish with freshly snipped chives.

Seared Sea Scallops with Artichoke Pesto

Sea scallops are so naturally rich and buttery that I wanted to create an appetizer that would highlight their fantastic flavor and texture. Making sure that they are just barely cooked through on the inside and nice and crispy on the outside is essential (see hint below.) I also whipped up a simple and incredibly delicious artichoke pesto, which lends a nice contrast in texture and color to the scallops.

GENEROUS TIP: Be sure to heat your pan over medium-high heat until very hot. This will probably take several minutes. To ensure a crispy sear, pat your scallops dry with paper towels. Do not overcrowd the pan—cook them in batches—otherwise your scallops will steam, not sear!

MAKE AHEAD: The pesto can be made ahead and refrigerated for up to 2 days.

SERVES 4 TO 6
PREP TIME: 10 MINUTES
COOK TIME: 5 MINUTES

1 pound sea scallops
    (10 to 15)

kosher salt and freshly
    ground black pepper

2 tablespoons olive oil

1 tablespoon unsalted butter

2 cloves garlic, smashed
    but left whole

micro greens, for garnish

ARTICHOKE PESTO

2 cloves garlic

1 cup roughly chopped
    fresh flat-leaf parsley

½ cup steamed fresh
    artichoke hearts
    (see page 36)

½ cup blanched almonds

½ cup grated Parmesan
    cheese

⅓ cup lemon juice

⅓ cup olive oil

kosher salt

1   First make the Artichoke Pesto: In the bowl of a food processor, combine the garlic, parsley, artichoke hearts, almonds and Parmesan. Pulse until combined but still chunky. With the machine running, stream in the lemon juice and olive oil. When the pesto is creamy, thick and bright green, season with salt. Set aside.

2   Rinse and drain the scallops. Pat dry and season both sides with salt and pepper.

3   Heat a 10-inch pan over medium-high heat. Add the olive oil, butter and smashed garlic cloves. As the garlic cloves begin to brown and flavor the oil, add the scallops to the pan—but only 5 to 6 at a time. Cook until browned on one side, about 1 minute, then sprinkle with salt and pepper. Flip the scallops over and cook until the scallops are still a little translucent in the middle and golden and a little crisp on the edges, about 2 minutes total.

4   Transfer the scallops to a serving dish with a dollop of pesto. Garnish with a little micro greens and serve immediately.

Zucchini Lemon Cupcakes

Every year, I push myself to come up with new zucchini recipes to make use of the dozens of freakishly large zucchinis that grow in my garden. Baking desserts is one of my favorite ways to use up veggies because it tricks my kids into eating vegetables they otherwise do not. As in my Chocolate Beet Cake (page 83) and Carrot Cake (page 65), vegetables add wonderful moisture and texture and are naturally sweet. I include a bit of lemon zest in this batter and the cream cheese frosting to add brightness.

MAKES 12 CUPCAKES
PREP TIME: 10 MINUTES
COOK TIME: 18 MINUTES

½ cup unsalted butter

1 cup sugar

2 large eggs

1 teaspoon vanilla extract

1½ cups shredded zucchini

zest of 1 lemon

1½ cups all-purpose flour

1 teaspoon baking soda

1 teaspoon baking powder

½ teaspoon salt

LEMON CREAM CHEESE FROSTING

½ cup (1 stick) salted butter, softened

8 ounces cream cheese

zest of 1 lemon, very finely minced

1 tablespoon fresh lemon juice

3 cups powdered sugar

1   Preheat the oven to 350°F. Prepare a 12-muffin tin with cupcake liners.

2   In the bowl of a standing mixer, combine the butter and sugar until well mixed. Add the eggs and vanilla and beat on medium-high until light and fluffy, about 2 minutes. Add the zucchini and lemon zest and mix on medium speed until the batter is uniform, about 2 minutes.

3   Meanwhile, in a separate bowl, combine the flour, baking soda and powder, and salt. Add the dry ingredients to the bowl of the mixer and combine to create a thick batter.

4   Divide the batter between the 12 muffin cups. Bake for 18 minutes, or until just golden brown on top and a toothpick stuck in the middle comes out clean.

5   Let the cupcakes cool slightly in the tin before transferring them to a cooling rack.

6   Meanwhile, make the Lemon Cream Cheese Frosting: In a standing mixer, beat together the butter and cream cheese. Add the lemon zest and juice and beat until fluffy. Add the powdered sugar, a little at a time, and beat everything into a light, fluffy frosting.

7   When the cupcakes are cooled completely, frost and serve!

Sugaring Edible Flowers for Garnish

I like to create pretty, edible garnishes for my cakes and cupcakes by sugar-coating edible flowers. Spray roses and pansies are my go-to flowers for this technique.

1   Line a sheet pan with parchment paper and arrange your flowers on the paper.

2   Whip an egg white until frothy and gently and lightly brush the egg white onto one flower or petal at a time, then sprinkle the egg white with granulated sugar. Put the sheet pan somewhere warm and dry and let the flowers dry overnight or up to several days.

Tea Party Shower

MENU

- RASPBERRY PEACH PROSSECO PUNCH

- BACON, PARMESAN AND CHIVE SCONES

- RED ONION JAM

- LEMON SCONES WITH RASPBERRIES

- LEMON COCONUT BISCUITS

- MERRIANN'S MELT-A-WAYS

- SUGAR COOKIES WITH BERRY FROSTING

- CARROT CAKE WITH VANILLA CREAM-CHEESE FROSTING

I am not sure I could even count the number of wedding and baby showers that I have been to or hosted in the last decade. Let's just say that it far exceeds the amount of fingers and toes I have! I love showers because they are such a beautiful way to celebrate a new chapter in someone's life. Whether it is an upcoming wedding or a friend's first little bundle of joy, showers make me silly with happiness. And because they are most often a gathering of women, I feel free to make them as over-the-top frilly and feminine as possible.

This shower was created for my sister-in-law Rachel when she was expecting her first child, my little niece Estelle. But the menu would be equally lovely for a wedding shower. I adore the notion of an old-fashioned tea party, and I like to host these types of parties in the late afternoon. You are off the hook from supplying your guests with a full meal, and also have a rare opportunity to pile on the sweets.

For the decorations, I used an assortment of charming tea pots and old cups and saucers that I have salvaged everywhere from my grandmother's cupboards to the Salvation Army. I love that they are all totally different, as they add tons of character. If you don't have a collection like this, I recommend borrowing from family and neighbors!

BUFFET WITH SCONES

There are a couple of rules I like to follow when setting up a buffet. My first rule is to incorporate different heights for visual interest and to highlight the shape or height of certain dishes. If it is a long buffet (like a kitchen island), I tend to cluster the highest platters in the center and let them taper out. If it is a shorter buffet (like a dining-room sideboard), I add height at the center and edges, with smaller plates interspersed.

The best way to get height is to stack pedestal dishes or cake plates. I stack two and even three on top of each other. Another way is to cover the buffet with a tablecloth, tucking stacks of books underneath. Place low platters or bowls on top of the stacks.

My second buffet rule is to keep the serving dishes somewhat consistent, either by choosing similar colors (such as all types of clear glass platters and bowls) or by texture (like vintage milk-glass cake plates). Years ago, I invested in eight inexpensive matching square white platters. I have used them again and again, as they always make my food displays look cohesive.

Raspberry Peach Prosecco Punch

There is something so wonderfully festive about an old-fashioned party punch, especially this one! Because of its beautiful color, I like to display it in a reproduction vintage glass drink dispenser (like the one on page 151) or a cool bowl or pitcher. Not only does it make a great visual display, it frees the hostess from having to serve everyone, making it easy for them to serve themselves.

SERVES 10
PREP TIME: 5 MINUTES

12 ounces frozen raspberries
2 cups peach nectar, chilled
1 bottle Prosecco, chilled
ice cubes

1 Put the frozen raspberries in a large glass pitcher or dispenser. Top with the peach nectar and Prosecco.

2 Fill the rest of the pitcher or dispenser with ice cubes. Stir and serve cold.

Bacon, Parmesan and Chive Scones

These savory scones are insanely good. They are so tender and creamy and packed with flavor. Serve them hot, with a pat of butter and a heaping spoonful of Red Onion Jam, and you have a great treat!

MAKES 8 SCONES
PREP TIME: 15 MINUTES
COOK TIME: 20 MINUTES

2 cups all-purpose flour

1 teaspoon baking powder

½ teaspoon baking soda

½ teaspoon salt

½ cup snipped chives

½ cup (1 stick) cold unsalted butter, cut into 1-inch pieces, plus additional for serving

1 cup finely grated Parmesan cheese

4 strips crispy bacon, chopped

⅔ cup heavy cream, chilled

1 large egg

Red Onion Jam (see below), for serving

1 Preheat the oven to 400°F. Line a sheet pan with a silpat liner or parchment paper.

2 In the bowl of a food processor, put the flour, baking powder and soda, salt and chives. Pulse to combine. Add the butter, Parmesan and bacon and pulse until the dough is a pea-like consistency.

3 In a separate bowl, whisk together the cream and egg.

4 Turn the food processor on and stream the cream and egg mixture into the dry ingredients. Mix just until the dough has formed a ball. This will be a wet sticky dough.

5 Turn the dough out onto a lightly floured surface and form into a disc. Cut the disc of dough into 8 even wedges and transfer to the prepared sheet pan.

6 Bake the scones for 10 minutes, until baked through and slightly golden on top. Transfer to a cooling rack until ready to serve.

7 Slice open the scones and serve hot with butter and Red Onion Jam, or at room temperature.

Red Onion Jam

This is made from caramelized red onions, cooked long and slow until they create a jam-like consistency. I love this as a spread on sandwiches, and it is especially delicious nestled with a pat of butter in the Bacon, Parmesan and Chive Scones (above).

MAKES 2 CUPS
PREP TIME: 2 MINUTES
COOK TIME: 45 MINUTES

3 tablespoons unsalted butter

2 red onions, thinly sliced against the grain

kosher salt

2 cups water

1 cup red wine

1 large sprig fresh thyme

1 tablespoon sugar

1 In a sauté pan over medium heat, melt the butter. Add the red onions and sprinkle with salt. Cook over medium heat, until slightly browned, about 5 minutes.

2 Add 1 cup of the water and, stirring often, cook the onions until the pan starts to dry up, about 10 minutes.

3 Add the wine, the remaining 1 cup water and the thyme sprig. Cook the onions until they are very soft and all of the liquid has all been cooked off, about 20 minutes.

4 When the onions are fairly dry and very soft, sprinkle with the sugar. Mix well and season with salt.

5 Discard the thyme sprig and refrigerate the jam for up to 5 days or until ready to use.

Lemon Scones with Raspberries

These scones just melt in your mouth. They are equally tender and creamy as the Bacon, Parmesan and Chive Scones (see page 59), but loaded with sweet and tart lemon and raspberry flavor. A lemon glaze drizzled over the top takes them to the next level. They make a wonderful afternoon snack or a luxurious breakfast that is actually quite fast and easy to prepare.

MAKES 8 SCONES
PREP TIME: 15 MINUTES
COOK TIME: 20 MINUTES

2 cups all-purpose flour

½ cup sugar

1 teaspoon baking powder

½ teaspoon baking soda

½ teaspoon salt

zest of 2 lemons

2 tablespoons fresh lemon juice

½ cup (1 stick) cold unsalted butter, cut into 1-inch pieces

⅔ cup plus 1 tablespoon heavy cream, chilled

1 large egg

½ cup raspberries

LEMON GLAZE

½ cup plus 3 tablespoons powdered sugar

2 tablespoons fresh lemon juice

1 tablespoon heavy cream

INGREDIENT NOTE: These are just as delicious without the raspberries —or with blueberries, strawberries or blackberries instead.

1   Preheat the oven to 400°F. Line a sheet pan with a silpat liner or parchment paper.

2   In the bowl of a food processor, put the flour, sugar, baking powder and soda, salt and lemon zest and juice and pulse to combine. Add the butter and pulse until the dough reaches a pea-like consistency.

3   In a separate bowl, whisk together ⅔ cup of the cream and the egg. Turn the food processor on and stream the cream and egg mixture into the dry ingredients. Mix just until the dough has formed a ball.

4   Turn the dough out onto a lightly floured surface and form into a disc. Slice in half horizontally and carefully open up like a hamburger bun. Sprinkle the raspberries onto the bottom half of the dough, and then place the top half on the raspberries, trapping them inside the dough.

5   Cut the dough into 8 even wedges and transfer to the prepared sheet pan. Using a pastry brush, lightly brush the tops of the scones with the remaining 1 tablespoon cream. Bake for 10 minutes, until baked through and slightly golden on top. Transfer to a cooling rack.

6   Meanwhile, make the lemon glaze: In a small bowl, whisk together the powdered sugar, lemon juice and cream until creamy and smooth.

7   Once the scones have cooled slightly, use a fork to drizzle the glaze over the tops of the scones. Serve warm or at room temperature.

Lemon Coconut Biscuits

These little cookies are reminiscent of English biscuits—not too sweet and perfect for afternoon tea. They are scented with lemon, and made moist and flavorful with shredded coconut. I roll them in sugar before they are baked, which gives the outside a nice crispy shell. The unusual addition of cream of tartar gives the inside a lightness that begs to be washed down with a cup of hot tea.

MAKES 18 COOKIES
PREP TIME: 10 MINUTES
COOK TIME: 10 MINUTES

⅔ cup shredded sweetened coconut

½ cup (1 stick) unsalted butter, softened

¾ cup brown sugar

1 large egg

1⅓ cups all-purpose flour

1 teaspoon cream of tartar

½ teaspoon baking soda

½ teaspoon salt

zest of 1 lemon

1 tablespoon fresh lemon juice

½ cup sugar

1 Preheat the oven to 350°F. Prepare 2 sheet pans with silpat liners or parchment paper.

2 In the bowl of a food processor, pulse the coconut until it is a very fine consistency. Set aside.

3 In the bowl of a standing mixer, cream together the butter and the sugar until fluffy. Add the egg and beat until fluffy.

4 In a separate bowl, combine the flour, cream of tartar, baking soda and salt. Add the dry ingredients to the batter and partially combine. Add the coconut, lemon zest and juice and beat until you have a thick dough.

5 Place the sugar in a shallow bowl. Using a 1-inch ice cream scoop and working in batches, scoop out balls of the cookie dough and put them into the bowl of sugar. Roll the dough balls in the sugar until covered completely with a light layer of sugar. Transfer to the prepared sheet pans.

6 Bake the cookies for 8 minutes, until golden. Transfer to a wire rack and serve hot or at room temperature.

Merriann's Melt-a-ways

Merriann is the mother of one of my dearest and oldest friends, Missy. She is not only one of the sweetest, kindest women I have ever met, but the quintessential mama. You almost want to get sick so that she will bring you homemade soup and make you milkshakes. Merriann also happens to be quite the cookie baker. I love many of her recipes, but this one has made the transition from being deeply entrenched in their family repertoire, to now being one of our family's favorites! These tiny sweet and crispy sandwich cookies are the perfect size for popping into your mouth!

GENEROUS TIP: These cookies are so great for any type of party or shower because you can color them to match the theme. Simply add whatever food coloring fits your color palette.

MAKE AHEAD: Get a head start on your cookie making by preparing the dough up to 2 days in advance.

MAKES 2 DOZEN
PREP TIME: 20 MINUTES
  (plus 30 minutes refrigeration time)
COOK TIME: 12 MINUTES

1 cup (2 sticks) salted butter, softened

1 cup all-purpose flour

½ cup powdered sugar

¾ cup cornstarch

FILLING

3 ounces cream cheese, softened

1 cup powdered sugar

1 teaspoon vanilla extract

1 drop of food coloring (optional)

1 Combine the butter, flour, powdered sugar and cornstarch in the bowl of a standing mixer. Mix until the dough is crumbly.

2 Transfer the dough to a sheet of plastic wrap. Wrap tightly and refrigerate for at least 30 minutes or until needed.

3 Preheat the oven to 350°F. Line a sheet pan with a silpat liner or parchment paper.

4 Remove the dough from the fridge and roll it into 1-inch balls. Place the balls onto the prepared sheet pan and lightly press them flat with your palm.

5 Bake the cookies for 12 minutes, or until still pale in color, but cooked through. Remove from the oven and let the cookies cool slightly.

6 While the cookies are baking, make the filling: In a medium bowl, combine the cream cheese, powdered sugar, vanilla and food coloring, if using. Using a hand mixer, beat on high speed until you have a fluffy frosting.

7 While the cookies are still slightly warm, frost every other one with a dollop of frosting. Top each frosted cookie with a second cookie to create a little sandwich. Let the cookies and frosting cool and firm up completely before moving the cookies.

8 Serve immediately or at room temperature.

Sugar Cookies with Berry Frosting

This is my signature sugar cookie recipe—similar to a butter cookie, but far more tender and flaky. These can be rolled and cut into any shape you want, and frosted with the Berry Frosting or with royal icing or butter cream. But sometimes I think they are best just sprinkled with sugar and baked until barely done and still pale in color. For photo, see page 63.

GENEROUS TIPS: These cookies are wonderful with the addition of any type of extract—my favorites are lemon, vanilla and almond. These can be baked plain, as well, to ice or sprinkle with white or colored sugars. You can divide the icing base up, adding different berries to the batches for a variety of flavors and colors. I like raspberries, strawberries or blackberries for their colors.

MAKE AHEAD: These freeze very well and can be made up to 3 weeks ahead. Just thaw and bring to room temperature before frosting.

MAKES 2 DOZEN
PREP TIME: 30 MINUTES
  (plus 20 minutes refrigeration)
COOK TIME: 10 MINUTES

1 cup (2 sticks) salted butter, softened

¾ cup powdered sugar, plus more for rolling out the dough

pinch of salt

2 large egg yolks

2¼ cups all-purpose flour

BERRY FROSTING

½ cup (1 stick) unsalted butter, softened

1½ cups powdered sugar

6 berries

1   In a standing mixer with the paddle attachment, cream the butter and sugar together until fluffy. Add the salt and the egg yolks and continue creaming. When they are well combined, add the flour and mix until just combined. It is important to not overmix, and it is okay if the dough is a little crumbly.

2   Turn the dough out onto a sheet of wax paper, and using the wax to help you, mold the dough into a disc. Refrigerate for at least 20 minutes or up to overnight.

3   Preheat the oven to 325°F. Line 2 baking sheets with a silpat liner or parchment paper.

4   Remove the dough from the refrigerator and turn out onto a surface lightly dusted with powdered sugar. Using a rolling pin, roll out the dough until it is ¼ inch thick, adding extra powdered sugar to keep the dough from sticking. Cut out rounds with a cookie cutter. Place the rounds on the prepared baking sheets.

5   Bake for 8 to 10 minutes, but be careful not to overbake. (I like these best before they have begun to brown.) Remove the cookies from the oven and cool for a few minutes on the sheet pans. Then carefully transfer them with a spatula to a cooling rack.

6   Meanwhile, make the berry icing: In a medium bowl, combine the butter, powdered sugar and berries and whip together until you have a smooth and fluffy frosting. Set aside at room temperature.

7   Frost the cookies only when they are completely cool.

Carrot Cake with Vanilla Cream Cheese Frosting

Now, please understand: This is a carrot cake for those people who normally do not like carrot cake. I know this because I am one of those people. There are no nuts or raisins or weird little bits of fruits in this cake. Or anything else that turns me off from your average carrot cake. This is just moist and tender, lightly spiced and completely delicious. It pairs so nicely with the frosting, which is creamy and light and flavored with vanilla with just a hint of tang from the cream cheese.

GENEROUS TIP: If you are a "normal" carrot cake lover, please feel free to add nuts and raisins and all those funny things you all like. For the frosting, if you cannot find vanilla paste, I recommend scraping out a vanilla bean to achieve maximum vanilla flavor and those gorgeous little black flecks from the seeds. However, plain old vanilla extract will achieve a perfectly lovely result, too.

SERVES 8 TO 10
PREP TIME: 20 MINUTES
COOK TIME: 25 MINUTES

1 cup (2 sticks) salted butter, softened

¼ cup vegetable oil

1 cup brown sugar

1 cup granulated sugar

3 large eggs

1 tablespoon vanilla extract

2½ cups all-purpose flour

2 teaspoons cinnamon

2 teaspoons baking soda

2 teaspoons baking powder

½ teaspoon salt

¼ teaspoon ground nutmeg

3 cups shredded carrots

fresh berries or sugared edible flowers (page 55), for garnish (optional)

VANILLA CREAM-CHEESE FROSTING

1 cup (2 sticks) unsalted butter, softened

8 ounces cream cheese, at room temperature

1½ teaspoons vanilla paste

4 cups powdered sugar

1 tablespoon whole milk

1 Preheat the oven to 350°F. Prepare three 8-inch-round cake pans (or two 9-inch cake pans) with circles of parchment paper and baking spray.

2 In the bowl of a standing mixer, cream the butter, oil and sugars until fluffy. Add the eggs and vanilla and mix until well combined.

3 In a separate bowl, combine the flour, cinnamon, baking soda and powder, salt, and nutmeg. Add the dry ingredients to the mixer and mix until well combined. Add the carrots and beat until thoroughly combined.

4 Evenly divide the cake batter between the three (or two) cake pans. Bake the cakes for 25 minutes, or until a toothpick inserted into the middle comes out clean.

5 Let the cake layers cool in the pans on a cooling rack. When the pans are cool enough that you can handle them, turn the layers out onto the rack, parchment paper down.

6 Meanwhile, make the vanilla cream-cheese frosting: Combine the butter, cream cheese, vanilla paste, powdered sugar, and milk in a bowl and mix with a hand mixer until completely combined and light and fluffy.

7 When the cake is completely cool, peel the parchment paper off of the cake rounds and place one round on a cake stand. Frost the cake, then add another cake round, a layer of frosting, and the third cake round, if using, before completely coating the outside of the cake. Garnish with fresh berries or edible sugared flowers and serve immediately or at room temperature.

CHAPTER TWO

Summer

Summer for our family means the children are out of school, so we are out working in the garden, at the farmers' market, going boating, fishing, picnicking and enjoying the sun in any way that we can. We also harvest all of our own tomatoes, herbs, cherries, apricots, plums and figs from our urban garden, which totally dictates the cooking that I do. There is incredible abundance this time of year, and we take full advantage of it. My mother and I spend a whole week canning our homegrown fruit every summer, and I delight in the never-ending fresh herbs and flowers! I also love the freedom and the casualness of summer entertaining. Everything can be done outdoors, which means there is way less cleanup and far more relaxation.

SUMMER MENUS

Boys' Breakfast

MENU

- SPICY BLOODY MARYS

- BUTTERMILK BANANA
  WAFFLES WITH
  MAPLE BUTTER SAUCE

- GREEN EGGS AND
  HAM BENEDICT

Pete works so hard and is such a great dad; sometimes it is nice to take an opportunity to spoil him. He rarely takes the time for a round of golf or a good soccer game anymore, so I like to send him off for a guilt-free day of fun with the boys after a good breakfast. The girls love to help, and may even pitch in with some homemade cards to his (and my) delight. They usually go something like this: "I love daddy because he takes me to pizza and plays games and gives me lovies." — Coco.

In my head, Food = Love, so if I am going to serve him a special breakfast, I want it to be something he really adores that will keep him full during a long busy day. Eggs Benedict is his unchallenged favorite breakfast item, followed by dressed-up waffles. And, frankly, hot coffee and Bloody Marys are not even debatable—they are a must.

Spicy Bloody Marys

My sister Julie always calls Bloody Marys the perfect drink because "they are a drink and a snack all in one." She is right, which is why I would drink this at any time of day. However, it is a traditional breakfast cocktail, and a favorite in our family (especially on Pete's side). We like them spicy and full of garnishes to snack on.

GENEROUS TIP: You could really go nuts with the garnishes. I like to include celery stalks, large green olives, tipsy pearl onions, spicy green beans and lemon or lime wedges for a start. But you could also include different salts for rimming the glass, as well as any other kind of garnish you like. And don't forget the hot sauce! For my take on the Bloody Mary bar, see page 151.

SERVES 6
PREP TIME: 5 MINUTES

46 ounces vegetable juice

¼ cup fresh lemon juice

½ cup prepared horseradish

1 teaspoon celery seeds

4 dashes Worcestershire
   sauce

1 cup vodka

kosher salt and freshly
   ground black pepper

ice cubes

1   In a large pitcher, combine the vegetable juice, lemon juice, horseradish, celery seeds and Worcestershire sauce. Mix really well.

2   Add the vodka and stir again. Season with salt and pepper.

3   Serve over ice and garnish as you desire.

Buttermilk Banana Waffles with Maple Butter Sauce

Waffles are one of the more nostalgic recipes from my youth. We had an unspoken weekend tradition that my dad made waffles every Saturday morning. To be clear—my dad doesn't cook. He BBQs salmon, and he makes waffles. He would whip up the batter and spoon it into our ancient round waffle maker. We kids loved it and squealed in delight as the first toasty golden waffle was split between us. And then, fast as he could, my dad would keep those waffles coming until he ran out of batter or we surrendered to our full little bellies. Now I make waffles for my own children, but every time I do, I think of my dad. I serve this version with fresh sliced bananas and a sprinkling of toasted pecans. Oh, and of course tons of Maple Butter Sauce.

SERVES 4 TO 6
PREP TIME: 15 MINUTES
COOK TIME: 10 MINUTES

2 eggs

½ cup (1 stick) butter

2 cups all-purpose flour

1 tablespoon sugar

2 teaspoons baking powder

1 teaspoon baking soda

1 teaspoon salt

2 bananas

½ cup sour cream

1½ cups buttermilk

toasted pecans for garnish

MAPLE BUTTER SAUCE
MAKES 1¾ CUPS

1 cup maple syrup

½ cup (1 stick) butter

3 tablespoons heavy cream

pinch of kosher salt

1　Preheat the waffle maker and grease with cooking spray.

2　Separate the eggs, reserving the yolks and adding the whites to a large clean bowl. Set aside.

3　Melt the butter in a small saucepan over medium-low heat and cook until golden brown. Set aside to cool slightly.

4　Combine the dry ingredients in a large bowl.

5　In a medium bowl, thotoughly mash the two bananas. Add the reserved egg yolks, sour cream and buttermilk and mix well. Add this wet mixture to the dry ingredients and mix well. Stir in the cooled butter.

6　Whisk the reserved egg whites in a clean bowl until they form stiff peaks. (This should take 2 to 3 minutes of whisking; alternatively you could use an electric mixer.) Gently fold the whites into the batter until completely incorporated.

7　Ladle the batter into the waffle maker and cook until the waffles are golden brown, 2 to 3 minutes. Repeat until all the batter is gone.

8　Meanwhile, make the maple butter sauce: In a small saucepan over medium heat, combine the maple syrup, butter, heavy cream, and salt, whisking until the butter is melted and the sauce is smooth. Simmer until the mixture is lightly bubbling and slightly thickened, about 3 minutes.

9　Serve the maple butter sauce hot with the warm waffles as they're ready.

Green Eggs and Ham Benedict

I couldn't help myself: I had to do a riff on Pete's favorite, old-fashioned eggs Benedict. But you know what? He actually enjoyed it so much that now he requests this over the regular version. The addition of spicy jalapeño, creamy avocado and Serrano ham take this Benedict to the next level.

GENEROUS TIP: When I was in culinary school, we were taught that using the blender for hollandaise sauce was only a fallback to salvage a broken sauce. Frankly, I must be lazy, because as soon as it occurred to me that making hollandaise in a blender is a sure thing every time, that is the only way I make it. Why worry? Just blend.

SERVES 4
PREP TIME: 10 MINUTES
COOK TIME: 5 MINUTES

JALAPEÑO HOLLANDAISE

½ cup (1 stick) unsalted butter

2 large egg yolks

1 fresh jalapeño, stemmed and roughly chopped

¼ cup fresh lemon juice

kosher salt

2 tablespoons white vinegar

8 large eggs

4 English muffins

2 avocados, thinly sliced

8 ounces Serrano ham

kosher salt

1   First make the jalapeño hollandaise: Melt the butter in a small pan. In a blender, combine the egg yolks and jalapeño. With the blender running, add the melted butter in a stream, and then the lemon juice. Blend the hollandaise until smooth and somewhat thick; it will be a pale green. Season with salt and set aside.

2   Bring a medium pot of water to a boil over medium heat. Add the white vinegar and, using a spoon, start swirling the water vigorously in a circle. When a mini whirlpool has formed in the center of the pot of water, gently ease two of the eggs in, one at a time. Cook the eggs for 2 minutes and then remove with a slotted spoon and set aside while you repeat with the remaining eggs. The eggs will be a tad undercooked, but right before serving, you just dip them back in the boiling water with a slotted spoon to heat them back up.

3   While the eggs are poaching, toast the English muffins.

4   On each half of a toasted English muffin, fan out an eighth of the avocado slices. Pile 1 ounce of the Serrano ham on top, then add one hot poached egg. Pour the jalapeño hollandaise over the top of the eggs and serve immediately with extra hollandaise on the side.

Southern Housewarming

MENU

- CHERRY MINT LEMONADE

- PEACH DANDY

- FRIED GREEN TOMATOES

- NATALIE'S NC SLAW

- SPICY PULLED PORK SANDWICHES WITH GRILLED RED ONIONS

- CHOCOLATE BEET CAKE

A few years ago, my little brother Jonny married a Southern Belle. Natalie is an incredible cook, who has taught our family to truly appreciate all kinds of Southern specialties. I mean, while we all loved bourbon, pulled pork and fried green tomatoes, Natalie has taught us to really savor them. Trust me when I say bourbon has become a staple beverage in our family.

When Jonny and Natalie bought their first house, there had to be a big celebration brimming with Southern-influenced dishes and hospitality. We set a king's table in their back yard, ate family style, and capped off the delicious spread with a bourbon tasting bar. For tips on how to set up your own liquor tasting bar, see opposite.

HOW TO SET UP A LIQUOR TASTING BAR

I would recommend offering between three and five varieties of whatever liquor you are featuring at your tasting. Arrange them with cards detailing their brand, origin, flavor profile and whatever other information you think your guests might like to know. You could use anything from small juice glasses, petite mason jars or shot glasses; stack them on the bar so that guests can help themselves to a taste. Good tasting liquors are bourbon, tequila and Scotch.

Cherry Mint Lemonade

A refreshing sweet and sour drink with a slight fizz and a lovely mint flavor, this lemonade is great for children and grownups alike. It has a gorgeous deep red color and is packed with freshly squeezed lemon juice, ripe cherries and garden-grown mint.

GENEROUS TIP: An "adult" version of this would be double-trouble delicious. Just add a few ounces of cold vodka!

SERVES 4 TO 6
PREP TIME: 10 MINUTES
COOK TIME: 2 MINUTES

2 cups cherries, pitted

6 large lemons

2 stalks fresh mint, plus 4 to 6 sprigs, for garnish

1 liter club soda, chilled

MINT SIMPLE SYRUP

½ cup sugar

½ cup water

8 large fresh mint leaves

1 First make the mint simple syrup: In a small pot, combine the sugar and water. Add the mint leaves. Bring to a simmer over medium heat, gently swirling the pot to cover the mint leaves. Simmer for 1 to 2 minutes, or until the sugar is dissolved.

2 Remove from the heat and let cool slightly before transferring the syrup to a blender.

3 Very carefully puree the sugar mixture on high speed until the mint leaves release all of their juice into the simple syrup and the syrup turns green. Pour the simple syrup through a small strainer and into a jar or heatproof bowl. Discard the mint solids. When completely cooled, transfer to an airtight container and keep in the refrigerator for up to 2 weeks or until ready to use.

4 Place the cherries in a blender and puree until you have a pretty smooth cherry puree.

5 Juice the lemons into a pitcher or bowl, straining for seeds. Add the cherry puree and the mint simple syrup and stir to combine.

6 In a large pitcher, add the stalks of fresh mint and lots of ice. Pour the cherry-lemon mixture over the ice. Fill the rest of the pitcher with the club soda and stir to combine.

7 Pour the lemonade into glasses and garnish each with a sprig of fresh mint.

Peach Dandy

This cocktail is pure summer. The sweet fresh peach puree and sour hit of lime juice make this drink very refreshing. The orange peach puree combined with the rose-colored blush of the grenadine also make this drink party pretty!

MAKES 1 COCKTAIL
PREP TIME: 5 MINUTES

ice cubes

2 tablespoons Simple Syrup (page 45)

1½ ounces vodka

¼ cup peach puree

2 tablespoons fresh lime juice

1 teaspoon grenadine

Fresh peach wedges, for garnish

1 In a cocktail shaker filled with ice, combine everything but the grenadine. Shake thoroughly and then strain into an ice-filled highball glass.

2 Tilt the glass a bit and add the grenadine (it will sink to the bottom of the glass).

3 Garnish with fresh peaches and serve immediately.

Fried Green Tomatoes

To me this is one of the dishes that epitomizes Southern food. Natalie taught me this recipe in her grandmother's old cast-iron skillet (which only enhanced my romantic notions of Southern food traditions.) I love to make a big crispy batch of these and serve them family style. They are also outstanding additions to sandwiches, especially a BLT!

MAKE AHEAD: These are great for entertaining because you can do half of the work the day before: The tomatoes can sit in the marinade in your refrigerator for up to 24 hours. Then you just dredge and fry them the day of your party.

GENEROUS TIPS: You could also cook these in bacon fat. (I know.) This would require cooking 1 pound of bacon, and keeping all of the fat in the pan until you are ready to fry the tomatoes.
    Use a fork to turn these tomatoes as they are frying. It is the gentlest way to handle them. If you try to use a spatula, you will wind up scraping the breading off of the tomatoes.

SERVES 4 TO 6
PREP TIME: 15 MINUTES
  (plus 1 to 24 hours for marination)
COOK TIME: 12 MINUTES

5 green tomatoes

⅓ cup vegetable oil

2 large sprigs fresh rosemary

kosher salt

MARINADE

3 cups buttermilk

1 teaspoon smoked paprika
  (hot smoked paprika optional)

4 dashes hot sauce

¼ teaspoon freshly ground
  black pepper

½ teaspoon onion powder

¼ teaspoon garlic powder

2 teaspoons kosher salt

BREADING

2 cups finely ground cornmeal

½ cup all-purpose flour

1 teaspoon smoked paprika
  (hot smoked paprika optional)

¼ teaspoon freshly ground
  black pepper

½ teaspoon onion powder

¼ teaspoon garlic powder

2 teaspoons kosher salt

1 Slice the ends off of the tomatoes, reserving them for another use. You should be able to get three slices out of the remaining tomato, each one about ¼ inch thick. Set aside.

2 In a large mixing bowl, mix together all of the marinade ingredients. Place the tomato slices in the marinade, making sure that they are covered completely. Place in the refrigerator to marinate for at least 1 hour and up to 24 hours.

3 In a 9 x 13-inch baking dish, gently combine all of the breading ingredients.

4 Preheat the oven to 350°F. Line a sheet pan with parchment.

5 In a heavy skillet or sauté pan over medium heat, heat the oil and rosemary for about 5 minutes; the rosemary infuses the oil with its scent and flavor. Reduce the heat to low to prepare for frying.

6 Remove the tomato slices from the marinade and shake off any excess. Gently pull each slice of tomato through the breading, coating both sides.

7 Cooking in batches, fry the tomatoes in the hot skillet over low heat, for about 3 minutes. Turn the tomatoes with a fork and cook on the other side for 3 minutes, until the tomatoes are firm in the middle, not mushy, and the breading is slightly crispy and golden. Transfer the hot tomatoes to the prepared sheet pan and immediately sprinkle with kosher salt.

8 When you have filled the sheet pan with the tomatoes, warm them in the preheated oven for about 5 minutes. Pile them onto a platter and serve hot immediately.

Natalie's N.C. Slaw

I have an aversion to mayonnaise. Everyone who knows me knows this. So, I have never been much of a traditional slaw fan—until my sister-in-law Natalie made a vinegar-based slaw that delighted and dazzled me! It is North Carolina style, as that is where she is from, and it is zippy, spicy, fresh and delicious. Not to mention, totally devoid of mayonnaise, which not only makes me excited but also means it can sit out in the hot summer sun with no worries! We pile this slaw on Pulled Pork Sandwiches, burgers or just enjoy it as a salad.

MAKE AHEAD: This is meant to sit for 24 hours before serving, which is an incredible advantage from the perspective of a hostess! When it is ready to serve, the cabbage will be very soft and there should be lots of extra liquid in the slaw.

SERVES 4 TO 6
PREP TIME: 15 MINUTES
   (plus 24 hours of refrigeration)

1 head green cabbage

1 bunch green onions

⅔ cup apple cider vinegar

2 tablespoons ketchup

2 tablespoons brown sugar

1 teaspoon red pepper flakes

kosher salt

1   Split the cabbage in half, and cut the core out of each half. Thinly slice the cabbage and place it in a large bowl.

2   Thinly slice the green onions, white and green parts, and add them to the bowl with the cabbage.

3   In a small bowl, combine the apple cider vinegar, ketchup, brown sugar and red pepper flakes. Season with salt.

4   Dress the cabbage and green onions and toss well to combine. Cover the bowl with plastic wrap and refrigerate the slaw for 24 hours.

5   Serve as a side dish or as a condiment for the Pulled Pork Sandwiches (see opposite).

Spicy Pulled Pork Sandwiches with Grilled Red Onions

You can prepare this dish and then walk away from it for hours while it simmers and gets more and more tasty. In other words, it's perfect for a busy schedule. I like to get this going and then get other things done while it cooks. The result is a slow-braised pulled pork that falls apart in your mouth. Layers of spice and aromatics take this fantastic sandwich filling over the edge.

GENEROUS TIP: I also use this versatile pulled pork as the base for tacos and pork chili. It yields about 8 cups pulled pork.

MAKES 6 SANDWICHES
PREP TIME: 20 MINUTES
COOK TIME: 4 HOURS

SPICY PULLED PORK

one 3½ pound pork shoulder

kosher salt

1 yellow onion, thinly sliced

one 10-ounce container fresh medium salsa

3 cloves garlic

3 oranges, cut in half

2 jalapeños, sliced

1 quart chicken broth

1 quart water

1 red onion, thickly sliced into rounds

2 tablespoons vegetable oil

kosher salt

6 brioche buns, sliced in half three-quarters through

Natalie's NC Slaw
  (see opposite)

1 First get the spicy pulled pork going: Put a large heavy pot over high heat. Season the pork generously with salt.

2 When the pot is really hot, after about 2 minutes, put the pork shoulder in the pot and sear the pork on all sides.

3 Add the onion, salsa, garlic, jalapeño and orange halves. Stir in the broth and then the water. Bring the liquid to a light boil, then turn the heat to low and put a lid on the pot. Simmer the pork for about 3 hours, or until falling apart.

4 Remove the pot from the heat. Transfer the pork shoulder to a cutting board. Return the cooking liquid to the stove over high heat. Boil the liquid until it has been reduced to a few cups, about 10 minutes. Discard the oranges.

5 While the cooking liquid is reducing, pull the meat away from the bone and shred it, discarding any bone or fat. Reserve the meat on the cutting board.

6 When the sauce is reduced, add the meat to the sauce and stir to combine. Season with salt. You can serve hot or refrigerate in an airtight container up to 3 days or until ready to use. (To reheat the Spicy Pulled Pork, place it in a baking dish covered in foil. Bake at 350°F for 20 minutes.)

7 To assemble the sandwiches, preheat a grill or grill pan over medium heat.

8 Put the red onion slices in a small bowl. Drizzle with the vegetable oil and a sprinkle of salt; toss to combine. Grill over medium heat until the onions are tender and slightly charred, about 5 minutes. Set aside.

9 Pile a generous amount of pork onto each brioche bun, and top with some grilled onions and a scoop of slaw. Serve immediately.

Chocolate Beet Cake

This is absolutely one of the best chocolate cakes I have ever had—and my husband's favorite. And, no, you did not read this wrong. It is chock full of beets. This recipe actually started as a daydream when I saw an insanely fluorescent purple cake—just like the juice that comes from a raw beet. I was so excited to bring this cake to life, but it turns out beets in baked goods come out a bit of a muddy reddish brown. I thought, why not take the moistness and earthy flavor of the beets and complement them with rich chocolate and a tiny touch of cinnamon? I added cocoa to the cake batter and the result was the most intensely moist and chocolaty cake I have ever had. I frosted the cake with a rich chocolate buttercream flavored with a touch of espresso.

MAKE AHEAD: The beet puree can be made up to several days ahead of time and kept in an airtight container in the refrigerator.

SERVES 10 TO 12
PREP TIME: 10 MINUTES
COOK TIME: 45 MINUTES

2 to 3 large beets

¾ cup (1½ sticks) salted butter, at room temperature

1½ cups granulated sugar

1½ teaspoons vanilla extract

3 large eggs

1½ cups all-purpose flour

1½ cups cocoa powder

1 teaspoon baking powder

1 teaspoon baking soda

½ teaspoon salt

½ teaspoon cinnamon

1 cup whole milk

CHOCOLATE BUTTERCREAM FROSTING

1 cup (2 sticks) salted butter, at room temperature

1 cup dark unsweetened cocoa powder

4 cups powdered sugar

⅓ cup strong coffee

1 tablespoon whole milk

1. Preheat the oven to 325°F. Prepare two 9-inch cake pans with baking spray and parchment paper rounds.

2. In a medium pot filled with simmering water, boil the beets for 15 to 20 minutes. When the beets are fork-tender, drain them and let them sit until cool enough to handle. Peel off the skin and trim off the tops. Chop the beets into large pieces and throw them in the food processor. Pulse the beets until they form a smooth puree. Refrigerate in an airtight container for up to a week, or until ready to use. You should have about 1¼ cups beet puree.

3. In the bowl of a standing mixer, beat the butter and sugar until light and fluffy. Add the vanilla and eggs and beat to combine. Add the beet puree and beat until well-combined. (It will look like the batter has curdled, but it is fine!)

4. In a separate bowl, add the flour, cocoa powder, baking powder, baking soda, salt and cinnamon and mix them all together. Add the flour mixture and the milk to the mixing bowl. Mix the batter on medium speed until it is completely combined and smooth, about 2 minutes.

5. Divide the batter evenly between the two cake pans. Bake for 25 minutes, or until a toothpick inserted in the center comes out clean.

6. Remove the cakes from the oven and let them cool in their pans on a rack.

7. Meanwhile, combine all of the chocolate buttercream frosting ingredients in the bowl of a standing mixer and whip until smooth and fluffy.

8. When the cake is completely cool, turn the layers out of their pans and place one of the cake rounds on a cake plate. Slather a generous amount of the frosting on the cake. Top with the second cake round and use the rest of the frosting to cover the top and sides of the cake.

9. Slice and serve.

Lake Picnic

MENU

- YELLOW NECTARINE MOJITOS

- COUSCOUS SALAD WITH
  CHERRIES AND FETA

- ROASTED PORK TENDERLOIN
  SANDWICH WITH ZESTY
  ROASTED RED PEPPER SPREAD

- RASPBERRY PEACH BARS

Clear and sparkling days do happen in Seattle—there are summer afternoons where there may be no more beautiful place on earth. You are surrounded by green- and blue-sprawling mountains, and everywhere you look there is water: the Puget Sound, rivers and several beautiful lakes. These are the days when you can't stand to be inside and everyone cuts out of work early to seek their own patch of grass to sprawl on. One afternoon we invited good friends on a picnic by a lake, and this was the meal that I packed. A rare evening just for grownups filled with delicious food, icy cold cocktails and a late sunset—pretty much heaven for overly tired parents.

THE MANY USES FOR MASON JARS

These are one of the most versatile items I have in my kitchen. They are my go-to pick for packing salads, fruit, pastas and even cobbler for a picnic. You can seal them tightly and throw them in a cooler for travel. They also create very cute and casual individual serving dishes or step in as fun glasses for juices or cocktails. I use them for shaking and storing salad dressing in my refrigerator. I even bake cakes and fruit crisps in mason jars, as they are heatproof. They are sold at almost every grocery store and are very inexpensive, which make them an even better choice.

Yellow Nectarine Mojitos

Mojitos are like gold in the summer. Beautiful, shiny and everyone wants one. Just keep these on ice and marvel at the sweet, fruity and refreshing cocktail that will keep for hours in a simple mason jar. They just get better as the nectarine, lime and mint flavors marinate together.

MAKES 1 COCKTAIL
PREP TIME: 5 MINUTES

½ cup necatarines, diced

6 fresh mint leaves,
   roughly torn

½ lime, sliced in half

1 tablespoon sugar

2 ounces white rum

2 ounces club soda, chilled

INGREDIENT NOTE: You can substitute peaches for the nectarines, or yellow cherries if you're lucky enough to find them in your area. Red cherries work, too. If cherries are out of season, feel free to use frozen ones; they will still taste very good.

1 In the bottom of a heavy drinking glass, combine the nectarines, mint, lime wedges and sugar. Use a muddler to smash them all together and release all of the oils and juices.

2 Fill the glass with ice cubes and then add the rum. Top off the mojito with the chilled club soda.

3 Stir well and serve immediately with a straw.

Couscous Salad with Cherries and Feta

I love grain salads in the summer. They keep well in the heat and are a blank slate for fresh summer flavors. For this salad, I chose couscous and incorporated sweet and tart bing cherries and salty feta cheese. Some fresh, mild curly parsley add just the right hit of green and the slivered almonds contribute great texture and flavor. This is an easy and very pretty salad that lets cherries shine in a savory way for once!

SERVES 4 TO 6
PREP TIME: 10 MINUTES
COOK TIME: 20 MINUTES

2 cups sweet red cherries

2 cups water

4 tablespoons olive oil

½ teaspoon kosher salt

2 cups couscous

3 tablespoons minced shallot

kosher salt

3 tablespoons red wine vinegar

½ cup minced fresh curly parsley leaves

½ pound feta cheese

⅛ cup slivered almonds

INGREDIENT NOTES: This recipe is also amazing when you substitute the couscous for orzo pasta or quinoa. Blueberries can also replace the cherries in a pinch!

1 Pit the cherries into a small bowl and let sit while you make the couscous. (Some of their juices will drain into the bowl.)

2 In a medium saucepan, bring the water, 1 tablespoon of the olive oil and salt to a simmer. Stir in the couscous. Cover the saucepan and remove from the heat. Let sit, covered, for about 15 minutes. Remove the lid and fluff with a fork. Let the couscous cool.

3 Slice the pitted cherries into thin rounds and set aside in another small bowl. Add the shallots to the juice in the first small bowl. Add a sprinkle of salt, the remaining 3 tablespoons olive oil and the vinegar. Mix together to create a dressing.

4 Add the dressing, along with ¼ cup of the minced parsley, to the couscous and gently toss to coat. Add the cherries and stir to combine. Crumble the feta cheese over the couscous and gently stir it in. Add the almonds and the remaining ¼ cup parsley and gently combine. Season with salt.

5 Serve the couscous salad at room temperature or chilled.

Roasted Pork Tenderloin Sandwich with Zesty Roasted Red Pepper Spread

This sandwich is hearty and exploding with flavor. It is piled high with tender roasted pork tenderloin, and then embellished with a bunch of toppings for maximum impact. I love the mild and chewy mozzarella, the peppery arugula and the garlicky, tangy red pepper spread that brings the whole sandwich to life. These are great made early in the day and then packed into the fridge where all of the flavors can meld and soak into the baguette.

SERVES 8
PREP TIME: 20 MINUTES
COOK TIME: 30 MINUTES

1 pork tenderloin

1 tablespoon olive oil

kosher salt and freshly
    ground black pepper

2 baguettes

12 ounces fresh mozzarella
    packed in water, drained

1 cup fresh arugula

½ cup Zesty Roasted Red
    Pepper Spread (see below)

**ZESTY ROASTED RED PEPPER
    SPREAD**

MAKES ½ CUP

4 ounces roasted red peppers
    packed in water, drained

¼ cup fresh flat-leaf
    parsley leaves

⅛ cup olive oil

3 tablespoons red wine
    vinegar

3 cloves garlic

kosher salt

1   Preheat the oven to 375°F. Line a sheet pan with tin foil.

2   Lay the pork tenderloin on the foil. Tuck the tapered end of the pork tenderloin under and drizzle the pork with the olive oil. Generously season with salt and pepper. Roast for 30 minutes, or until the juices run clear.

3   Meanwhile, make the red pepper spread: In the bowl of a food processor, combine all of the ingredients. Pulse until the garlic is well chopped and the spread has a thick but uniform consistency. Transfer to a small bowl and refrigerate in an airtight container for up to 3 days, or until needed.

4   Remove the pork from the oven and lest rest for 5 to 7 minutes before thinly slicing.

5   Slice each baguette in half, and then slice each piece in half horizontally. Evenly spread the zesty roasted red pepper spread on each of the 8 pieces of baguette. On the bottoms of the baguettes, evenly distribute the mozzarella followed by the pork, and then top with the fresh arugula. Replace the baguette tops and slice each sandwich in half again to make 8 sandwiches.

6   Serve immediately or wrap in parchment paper and refrigerate for up to 24 hours, or until ready to eat.

Raspberry Peach Bars

My mom's aunt Patience, affectionately known as Auntie Pitts, created some amazing recipes that I have come across in the family recipe archives. One of my favorites is for a shortbread bar. She tops it with chocolate and nuts, but I found a way to retool these shortbread bars for summer by topping them with fruit instead. I included a layer of sweet raspberry jam to protect the crust from sogginess and to add another dimension of flavor. The crumbly streusel-like topping is the crowning glory of these delectable fruit bars.

GENEROUS TIPS: Any combination of fresh summer fruit would be wonderful with these. My other favorite combinations are blackberry/peach, apricot/cherry and raspberry/rhubarb. I have found that it is a wise idea to put the 9 x 13 x 2-inch pan on a larger sheet pan as the fruit has a tendency to drip over the edges and make a mess on the bottom of your oven. No one wants to deal with cleaning that up.

MAKES 12 BARS
PREP TIME: 15 MINUTES
COOK TIME: 35 MINUTES

1 cup (2 sticks) unsalted butter, at room temperature

1 cup brown sugar

1 large egg yolk

½ teaspoon salt

1 teaspoon vanilla extract

2¼ cups all-purpose flour

⅔ cup raspberry jam

3 cups raspberries

3 cups sliced peaches

¼ cup sugar

2 tablespoons cornstarch

CRUMBLE TOPPING

6 tablespoons cold unsalted butter, cut into small pieces

½ cup brown sugar

⅔ cup all-purpose flour

¼ teaspoon cinnamon

1 Preheat the oven to 350°F, and prepare a 9 x 13 x 2-inch sheet pan with baking spray and parchment paper.

2 In the bowl of a standing mixer, combine the butter and brown sugar and mix together until fluffy. Add the egg yolk, salt and vanilla and mix until well combined. Add 2 cups of the flour and mix until well combined.

3 Turn the dough out onto the sheet pan and evenly spread it on the bottom of the pan, pressing it firmly with your hands. It will be thin, but it should spread to the edges.

4 Using an offset spatula or the back of a spoon, spread the raspberry jam in a thin layer over the dough.

5 In a medium bowl, combine the raspberries, peaches, sugar, remaining ¼ cup of flour and the cornstarch. Gently toss together and pour over the dough and jam.

6 Make the crumble topping: In another medium bowl, combine the cold butter pieces, brown sugar, flour and cinnamon. Using either a pastry cutter or clean hands, mix to combine, cutting the butter into the dry ingredients. When you have a crumble that is the consistency of peas, sprinkle it over the top of the fruit.

7 Bake the bars for 45 to 50 minutes, until the crumble topping is golden and the fruit is bubbling.

8 Let the bars cool completely before slicing.

Big Family Birthday

MENU

- BLACKBERRY JALAPEÑO MARGARITAS

- COLD GREEN BEAN SALAD WITH CHILE RELISH

- BLT PASTA

- SWEET AND SPICY PINEAPPLE BARBEQUED CHICKEN

- BLACKBERRY SHORTCAKES

- STRAWBERRY LEMONADE CAKE

I was raised in a family of four children. But something funny happened as we all grew up—we multiplied! Everyone got married and started having children. And then I married my husband, who was one of three boys, and they are all married and have children! It makes for a pretty hectic family schedule, especially when it comes to birthday parties. We have learned to group some of the birthdays together for everyone's sanity. Late July is a perfect example, as my older brother Chris and my oldest nephew Jake have birthdays within a few days of each other. I took full advantage of the gorgeous summer weather and threw the party outside, served buffet style so people could go and seat themselves out on the terrace. I included two desserts, birthday cake and shortcakes (since my brother adamantly "does not like cake") and kicked off the festivities with Blackberry Jalapeño Margaritas made with the blackberries my niece and I pick each summer.

I used simple linens and plain white plates for the table, but created centerpieces out of fresh summer produce, most of which is grown in my backyard. If you don't have your own garden, look to your local farmers' markets for inspiration.

CREATING A SUGAR RIM FOR A DRINK

This is a fun way to dress up anything from a cocktail, a glass of champagne or a juice drink. You simply take a lemon or lime wedge and rub it on the rim of the glass. Turn it upside down and press it into a dish of whatever you want to stick to the rim. Don't feel confined to using granulated sugar! I've created rims with colored sugars, sprinkles, non pareils, coconut and cocoa powder. Use your imagination!

Blackberry Jalapeño Margaritas

This is completely inspired by the Jale Berry Martini they serve at the Bazaar/SLS hotel in LA. I went there for a girlfriend's bachelorette party a couple of years ago. The only catch was that I was significantly pregnant. I longingly watched my gorgeous, skinny girlfriends sling back to-die-for cocktails while I nursed my decaf iced tea. But I allowed myself the lone sip (or two) of my girlfriend's Jale Berry Martini and was totally floored. It was a mixture of gin, blackberry and jalapeño and other secret stuff—but those were the flavors that stuck. So, this past summer, when I thought to swap out my traditional lime margaritas for blackberry ones, the jalapeño part jumped into my mind and this outlandish, totally delicious cocktail was born.

SERVES 4
PREP TIME: 10 MINUTES
COOK TIME: 2 MINUTES

large crystal sugar,
  for rims

¾ cup tequila

½ cup triple sec

½ cup freshly squeezed
  lime juice

1 cup Blackberry Jalapeño
  Syrup (see below)

ice cubes

fresh blackberries and
  lime wedges, for garnish

BLACKBERRY JALAPEÑO SYRUP

MAKES 1⅔ CUP

1 cup sugar

1 cup water

1 cup fresh blackberries
  or frozen blackberries,
  thawed

2 jalapeño peppers,
  minced

1 First make the syrup: Combine the sugar and water in a small pot and bring to a brief boil over medium heat.

2 Transfer to a blender and add the blackberries and jalapeños. Blend until smooth. To extract the seeds, pour through a fine-mesh strainer into an airtight container or mason jar. Refrigerate for up to a week.

3 Make the cocktails: Rim 4 glasses with the large crystal sugar (see Creating a Sugar Rim for a Drink, page 93) and fill with ice.

4 Fill a cocktail shaker with the tequila, triple sec, lime juice and blackberry jalapeño syrup, plus a handful of ice. Shake vigorously and strain the margaritas into the prepared glasses.

5 Garnish with fresh blackberries and lime wedges and serve.

Cold Green Bean Salad with Chile Relish

This cold green-bean dish is a nice departure from a traditional green salad. I love to make it during the warm months (and I find that the children are more prone to eat green beans than lettuce, too!). Make this salad in the morning, cover the bowl with plastic wrap and put in the refrigerator until lunch or dinner. It benefits from marinating in the relish for several hours, and tastes great cold or at room temperature. Double the recipe if you want to make it for a large group!

MAKE AHEAD: This salad tastes much better if you prepare it in the morning and refrigerate it, covered, until ready to serve.

SERVES 4 TO 6
PREP TIME: 10 MINUTES
   (plus 2 optional hours refrigeration)
COOK TIME: 3 MINUTES

kosher salt

1 pound green beans, trimmed

3 tablespoons minced shallots

2 tablespoons minced fresh flat-leaf parsley leaves

1 tablespoon whole-grain mustard

1 teaspoon minced red chile pepper

2 tablespoons red wine vinegar

2 tablespoons olive oil

1   Bring a large pot of salted water to a boil. Fill a large bowl with ice and water and keep it nearby.

2   Add the green beans to the boiling water and cook for 3 minutes, or until tender but still with some crunch. Drain and plunge the green beans into the ice bath until cold. Drain and set aside.

3   In a small bowl, combine the shallots, parsley, mustard, chile pepper, vinegar, and olive oil and mix well. Season with salt.

4   Place the green beans on a serving platter and top with the chile relish. This tastes best after it's been refrigerated for a few hours.

BLT Pasta

I created this delicious dish for last-minute dinner guests with the meager supplies I happened to have around: six slices of bacon, a box of spaghetti and two lemons. Luckily I had everything else growing in my garden. Basically this was made from scraps, but it is a masterpiece as far as I am concerned and we eat it all the time now. It has all of the charm of a BLT sandwich (Bacon- Lettuce- Tomato) only in a pasta. While this tastes best served immediately, it's super easy and quick to make.

SERVES 4 TO 6
PREP TIME: 10 MINUTES
COOK TIME: 20 MINUTES

kosher salt

1 pound spaghetti

6 slices thick-cut bacon

2 cloves garlic, minced

juice of 2 lemons

¼ cup olive oil

3 cups fresh arugula leaves

1 handful fresh basil leaves

2 cups cherry tomatoes

freshly ground black pepper

INGREDIENT NOTES: If you don't have cherry tomatoes, use larger tomatoes simply cut into bite-sized pieces. Just make sure they are ripe.

1 Bring a large pot of salted water to a boil.

2 Meanwhile, fry the bacon in a skillet over medium heat until crispy. Set aside to drain on a paper towel. Reserve the pan with the bacon fat.

3 Cook the pasta according to the package's directions.

4 In a small bowl, combine the garlic, lemon juice and olive oil to create a simple sauce. Pour into the reserved pan and bring to a simmer over medium heat.

5 When the pasta is done, drain it, then toss it with the hot dressing in the pan. Chop the reserved bacon and add it to the pasta along with the arugula, basil and cherry tomatoes. Toss to combine.

6 Season with salt and pepper and transfer to a platter. Serve immediately.

Sweet and Spicy Pineapple Barbequed Chicken

Barbequed chicken has been a summer favorite in my family since I was a child. I have very fond memories of my mom stewing up big pots of homemade BBQ sauce on the stove while my dad headed out to the grill with the chicken. I still love the process of making that big pot of sauce and letting it simmer on the stovetop, enjoying the intoxicating scent of tomato and spices. In this recipe, I add a unique and sweet twist by including ripe and juicy pineapple used two ways: cooked right into the sauce and grilled and served alongside the chicken.

SERVES 4 TO 6
PREP TIME: 15 MINUTES
COOK TIME: 1 HOUR AND 20 MINUTES

4 pounds chicken pieces

⅛ cup vegetable oil

kosher salt and freshly ground black pepper

half of a fresh pineapple, trimmed, cored, and cut into strips (save the second half for below)

PINEAPPLE BBQ SAUCE

⅛ cup vegetable oil

½ large yellow onion, roughly chopped

2 garlic cloves, chopped

1 large jalapeño pepper, minced (include seeds and veins)

½ teaspoon kosher salt, plus more for seasoning

one 28-ounce can diced tomatoes

one 20-ounce bottle of ketchup

½ cup cider vinegar

½ cup brown sugar

⅓ cup molasses

⅓ cup brandy

2 tablespoons Worcestershire sauce

2 cups fresh pineapple chunks (from second half of pineapple, above)

1. First make the pineapple BBQ sauce: In a large pot, heat the vegetable oil over medium-high heat. Add the onion and cook until it starts to soften, 3 to 5 minutes. Reduce the heat to medium, add the garlic and jalapeño and sprinkle them with the salt. Fry for about 5 minutes, or until the vegetables are soft. Add the tomatoes and cook for 5 to 7 minutes, or until the mixture reaches a simmer. Stir in the ketchup, vinegar, brown sugar, molasses, brandy and Worcestershire sauce. Finally, add the fresh pineapple chunks, cover, and simmer for about 20 minutes, until everything is soft and well combined.

2. Uncover the pot and cook for an additional 5 minutes. Remove the pot from the heat and let cool slightly.

3. Using a hand blender (or transfer to a regular blender in batches), puree the sauce until very smooth. Season with salt and refrigerate until needed. (This can be made up to several days ahead of time).

4. When ready to prepare the dish, preheat the grill to medium.

5. Toss the chicken pieces with the vegetable oil and generously season with salt and pepper.

6. Put the chicken on the grill and cook slowly, turning often, until the skin is crispy and the juices run clear, about 20 minutes. (The thighs and wings will be done before the breast pieces.)

7. In the last few minutes of cooking the chicken, add the pineapple strips to the grill and baste the chicken with the BBQ sauce.

8. When the chicken is fully cooked, baste it with the sauce again and pile it onto a platter with the grilled pineapple. Serve the extra sauce on the side.

Blackberry Shortcakes

The most important part of fruit shortcake (besides starting with beautiful fruit, of course!) is the texture of the shortcake. I wanted the moist, sweet flavor of a cake mixed with the buttery, flakiness of a pastry—and it was quite a process to find the exact combination! But this recipe makes perfect shortcakes. They are so moist on the inside they will almost seem like they are not cooked. And the tops are crispy like biscuits with a nice sugary crust. Paired with a vanilla-scented whipped cream and freshly picked blackberries, these are a heavenly treat, and the top summer dessert choice for many of our close friends and family.

SERVES 4
PREP TIME: 40 MINUTES
COOK TIME: 12 MINUTES

4 cups fresh blackberries, stems removed, plus more for garnish

6 tablespoons sugar

2 cups all-purpose flour

2 teaspoons baking powder

½ teaspoon salt

½ cup (1 stick) cold unsalted butter, cut into small pieces

½ cup plus 1 tablespoon heavy cream, chilled

1 teaspoon vanilla extract

2 teaspoons large crystal sugar

VANILLA WHIPPED CREAM

1½ cups heavy cream, chilled

2 tablespoons powdered sugar

1 teaspoon vanilla paste or vanilla extract

1 In a bowl, combine the blackberries with 3 tablespoons of the sugar and let macerate for about 30 minutes.

2 Preheat the oven to 425°F. Line a sheet pan with a silpat liner or parchment paper.

3 In the bowl of a food processor, place the flour, the remaining 3 tablespoons sugar, the baking powder and salt. Pulse to combine. Pulse in the cold butter and keep pulsing until the dough has a coarse crumb texture.

4 In a separate bowl, combine ½ cup cream and the vanilla. Add this to the wet ingredients and pulse to combine. The dough will be moist and crumbly.

5 Dump the dough out onto a lightly floured surface. Press the dough together with your hands until it barely forms a disc. Cut it into 4 pieces, and gently form them into circles. Place the shortcakes on the prepared sheet pan and gently brush the tops with the remaining 1 tablespoon cream. Sprinkle them with the large crystal sugar.

6 Bake the shortcakes for 12 minutes. Remove them from the oven and let cool slightly before cutting them in half horizontally.

7 While they are cooling, make the vanilla whipped cream: Add the cold cream to a large bowl. With an electric mixer, mix the cream on medium speed until it begins to get frothy and thick, about 1 minute. Sprinkle in the powdered sugar and add the vanilla extract. Mix on high speed until the cream holds a soft peak.

8 Place each shortcake on its own plate, or all of them on a serving platter. Remove the top of each shortcake and spoon about ½ cup of the macerated blackberries onto the bottom of the cake (this way the juice will really sink into the cake). Top the berries with a big dollop of whipped cream, and another spoonful of blackberries. Place the tops on each shortcake and serve immediately.

Strawberry Lemonade Cake

This cake was such an obvious request from the little girls in our family, the brainchild of my two girls and my niece Madison. When I asked them about their favorite treat for a hot summer day, they blurted out "pink lemonade!" and I went ahead and turned it into a cake: two layers of tart lemon cake sandwiched between layers of strawberry buttercream frosting and freshly sliced strawberries (girls like drama!). It is quite pretty, and I do have to say, the flavor is certainly reminiscent of a lovely glass of strawberry lemonade, just a bit more decadent!

SERVES 12
PREP TIME: 20 MINUTES
COOK TIME: 30 MINUTES

1 cup (2 sticks) unsalted butter, at room temperature

1¾ cups sugar

2 tablespoons fresh lemon zest

2½ cups all-purpose flour

1 teaspoon baking powder

1 teaspoon baking soda

½ teaspoon salt

4 large eggs

⅓ cup fresh lemon juice

1 cup buttermilk

8 to 10 large strawberries, hulled and sliced

STRAWBERRY BUTTERCREAM FROSTING

1 cup (2 sticks) unsalted butter, softened

5 cups powdered sugar

2 tablespoons whole milk

2 large strawberries, chopped

1. Preheat the oven to 350°F, with a rack in the middle. Prepare two 9-inch round pans with baking spray.

2. In the bowl of a standing mixer fitted with a whisk attachment, place the butter, sugar and lemon zest. Beat until light and fluffy.

3. In a separate bowl, mix together the dry ingredients and set aside.

4. With the mixer on low speed, add the eggs, one at a time, combining thoroughly in between. With the mixer still running, add the lemon juice (the batter will look curdled, but it's not!).

5. Add one third of the dry ingredients and ½ cup of the buttermilk. Mix, then stop and scrape the sides of the bowl. Repeat, adding another third of the dry ingredients and the remaining ½ cup buttermilk. Mix, then stop and scrape. Add the remaining third of the dry ingredients and mix until completely combined and the batter is light and fluffy.

6. Divide the batter evenly between the prepared pans. Bake the cakes for 25 to 30 minutes, or until a toothpick inserted in the center of a cake comes out clean. Let the cakes cool before removing them from the pans.

7. While the cakes are cooling, make the strawberry buttercream frosting: Combine the butter and powdered sugar in a large bowl or standing mixer. Mix together on medium speed until pale and fluffy, about 3 minutes. Add the milk and the strawberries and mix on high speed until the frosting is very fluffy and pale pink in color, with flecks of strawberry.

8. Invert one of the cake rounds onto a cake plate; generously spread with frosting and top with strawberry slices. Repeat with the remaining layer of cake and frosting. Frost the sides of the cake. Put in the refrigerator for about 30 minutes to allow the frosting to set.

9. Serve at room temperature.

Backyard BBQ

MENU

- RICK'S GUINNESS MARGARITAS

- CROSTINI WITH CHERRY
  TOMATOES, BASIL AND MINT

- CROSTINI WITH PEACHES,
  BLUE CHEESE AND HONEY

- CROSTINI WITH SPICY TAPENADE,
  GOAT CHEESE AND ROASTED
  PEPPERS

- TOMATOES STUFFED
  WITH FRESH CORN
  AND MANGO SALAD

- GRILLED WILD SALMON WITH
  APRICOT MUSTARD GLAZE
  AND STONE FRUIT

- POTATO SALAD WITH
  MUSTARD AND BACON

- PEACH COBBLER

- S'MORES CAKE

This is an old-fashioned backyard BBQ with a slightly untraditional menu. We try to organize one of these every summer. I like to create a menu full of seasonal produce with some fresh takes on standard BBQ recipes like corn, potato salad and campfire s'mores. Everything here is meant to be set out buffet style so the guests serve themselves and the hostess gets to have fun. We like to set up picnic tables or set out piles of blankets so that families can spread out on the lawn with their plates. The atmosphere is casual and we are sure to put out lots of fun games to entice the kids to run around on the lawn.

CREATIVE DRINK COOLERS

There are so many really cool and unique ways to set out chilled drinks for self service. Forget the coolers! Instead, fill one of these containers with drinks and tons of ice: your wheelbarrow, the kitchen sink, brightly colored laundry tubs, ceramic or plastic planters and pots, giant clamshells, galvanized tin tubs and pails, and (one of my very favorites!) an outdoor fountain.

Rick's Guinness Margaritas

When you read this ingredient list, you will probably not believe that these will turn out to be some of the best (and most unique) margaritas you will ever try! Our friend Rick introduced these to us years ago, and we break this crazy recipe out several times every summer, much to everyone's delight. Watch out—they are potent!

SERVES 8
PREP TIME: 5 MINUTES

one 12-ounce can limeade
  concentrate

12 ounces tequila

6 ounces triple sec

three 14-ounce cans
  Guinness, chilled

2 limes, sliced into rounds

1 liter club soda, chilled

1 Add the limeade concentrate to a large pitcher filled with ice.

2 Refill the empty can with tequila and add it to the pitcher.

3 Now fill the can halfway with triple sec and add it to the pitcher. Add the three cans of Guinness and the limes and mix well. Top off the pitcher with the chilled club soda and mix again.

4 Serve immediately.

Crostini with Cherry Tomatoes, Basil and Mint

I remember the first time I ate bruschetta: I was a teenager at a friend's party and it was a piece of toasted baguette piled high with a mixture of tomatoes, basil and garlic, which had been drowned in balsamic vinegar and olive oil. It was the first way that I learned to enjoy raw tomatoes and that moment still sticks with me as it opened my mind up to the millions of possibilities that tomatoes offer. I've tried to pay homage to that simple tomato and basil bruschetta with this elevated version of the classic that uses garden-fresh summer ingredients.

SERVES 4 TO 6
PREP TIME: 10 MINUTES
COOK TIME: 7 MINUTES

twelve ¼-inch-thick
   slices baguette

4 tablespoons olive oil

1 garlic clove

1 pint cherry tomatoes,
   cut in half

3 tablespoons thinly
   sliced fresh basil leaves

2 tablespoons thinly
   sliced shallot

2 tablespoons thinly
   sliced fresh mint

2 tablespoons olive oil

1 tablespoon red
   wine vinegar

kosher salt

1   Preheat the oven to 400°F.

2   Place the baguette slices on a sheet pan and drizzle with 2 tablespoons of the olive oil. Bake for about 7 minutes, or until golden brown.

3   Remove the pan from the oven and rub the tops of the toasts with the raw garlic cloves. Set aside.

4   In a medium bowl, combine the cherry tomatoes, basil, shallot, mint, remaining 2 tablespoons of olive oil and the vinegar. Toss gently and season with salt.

5   Evenly distribute the topping among the crostini and transfer to a platter. Serve immediately.

Crostini with Peaches, Blue Cheese and Honey

These crostini are a wonderful mixture of sweet and savory flavors. I love the juicy peaches and the melted blue cheese drizzled with honey. And, while the fresh ripe peaches of the summer season are ideal, these are also easy to make with frozen peaches in the middle of the winter!

SERVES 4 TO 6
PREP TIME: 10 MINUTES
COOK TIME: 12 MINUTES

twelve ¼-inch-thick
  slices baguette

2 tablespoons olive oil

1 garlic clove

8 ounces Cambozola cheese

1 peach, sliced into
  12 thin wedges

2 tablespoons honey

INGREDIENT NOTE: Cambozola is a German soft ripened triple-cream cows' cheese. It is like a luscious brie streaked with blue veins. One of my favorites, it is widely available.

1 Preheat the oven to 400ºF.

2 Place the baguette slices on a sheet pan and drizzle with the olive oil. Bake for about 7 minutes, or until golden brown. Remove the pan from the oven and rub the tops of the toasts with the raw garlic clove. Set the toasts aside but leave the oven on.

3 Divide the cheese among the toasts and place 1 peach slice on top of each crostino. Return the sheet pan to the oven for 3 to 5 minutes, until the cheese is starting to melt and the peach slices have softened a little bit.

4 Transfer the toasts to a platter. Drizzle with the honey and serve immediately.

Crostini with Spicy Tapenade, Goat Cheese and Roasted Peppers

The Mediterranean flavors of these toasts are awesome. Creamy, tangy goat cheese and spicy, salty tapenade is topped with sweet roasted peppers for a fantastic and very easy appetizer. To make it even easier, prepare the tapenade ahead of time; it can be refrigerated for up to five days.

MAKE AHEAD: You could make the tapenade up to 5 days ahead of time.

SERVES 4 TO 6
PREP TIME: 15 MINUTES
COOK TIME: 7 MINUTES

twelve ¼-inch-thick
    slices baguette

2 tablespoons olive oil

8 ounces goat cheese,
    at room temperature

4 ounces roasted peppers
    packed in water, drained
    and thinly sliced

SPICY OLIVE TAPENADE

3 small garlic cloves

1 teaspoon orange zest

¼ teaspoon red
    pepper flakes

1 pint kalamata olives

2 teaspoons fresh oregano
    leaves

2 tablespoons olive oil

1　Preheat the oven to 400°F.

2　Place the baguette slices on a sheet pan and drizzle with the olive oil. Bake for about 7 minutes, or until golden brown. Remove the sheet pan from the oven and rub the tops of the toasts with the raw garlic clove. Set aside.

3　While the toasts are in the oven, make the spicy olive tapenade: In the bowl of a food processor, mince the garlic cloves. Add the orange zest, red pepper flakes, olives and oregano and pulse. Add the olive oil and pulse until you have a chunky spread. Refrigerate for up to 5 days, or until needed.

4　When you're ready to assemble the crostini, evenly divide the goat cheese among the toasts. Pile each toast with 1 tablespoon of the tapenade and top with the roasted peppers. Transfer to a platter and serve immediately.

Tomatoes Stuffed with Fresh Corn and Mango Salad

I love a good boiled or grilled corn on the cob, but where fresh corn really shines is in its raw state. It is so crunchy and with every bite, the kernels burst with surprisingly sweet and juicy corn milk. Here I use it as the base of a cold salad and add ripe chunks of mango to amp up the sweetness. Green onion, tomato, jalapeño, lime juice and fresh herbs add a variety of flavors and colors. Serving the salad in summer tomatoes is great for entertaining, but I also serve it in mason jars for casual gatherings.

GENEROUS TIPS: I cut my corn on a dishcloth; it keeps the kernels from bouncing around after they have been sliced off of the cob. I also like to use a serrated knife—it makes cutting kernels off of the cob easier. If you don't have fresh chive blossoms, use a different edible flower such as nasturtium or pansy petals

SERVES 6
PREP TIME: 25 MINUTES

6 large heirloom tomatoes

kosher salt and freshly ground black pepper

4 ears fresh raw corn, shucked and cleaned

½ mango, peeled and diced

½ bunch green onions, thinly sliced

½ cup cherry tomatoes, sliced in half

¼ cup minced fresh cilantro leaves

½ jalapeño pepper, finely minced

1½ tablespoons olive oil

3 tablespoons fresh lime juice

fresh chive blossoms, for garnish

1   Using a sharp paring knife, cut the tops off the tomatoes, and then gently cut around the edge of the inside of the tomatoes. Use a spoon or your hands to scoop out most of the inside of the tomatoes (reserve them for another use or discard), creating a cup. Sprinkle the insides of the tomatoes with salt and pepper.

2   Cut all of the corn kernels off of the cobs and place them in a large bowl. Add the mango, green onions, cherry tomatoes, cilantro, jalapeño, olive oil and lime juice. Gently mix to combine, then season with salt.

3   Spoon generous amounts of the corn salad into the tomato cups and transfer to a platter. Garnish with the chive blossoms and serve at room temperature, or refrigerate until chilled.

PERFECT LEMONADE

My secret to perfect lemonade it to make a symple syrup first. Simmer 1 cup sugar with 1 cup water and ¼ cup honey over low heat for about 2 minutes, or the sugar and honey is dissolved. Transfer to a glass bottle or plastic container and refrigerate until cold. To make a pitcher of lemonade, fill the pitcher with ice cubes. Add the simple syrup with 1 cup fresh lemon juice and 4 cups cold water and mix together well. Garnish with fresh lemon slices and fresh mint leaves. As you can see in the photo, this is a favorite of my daughters and a pitcher goes fast!

Grilled Wild Salmon with Apricot Mustard Glaze and Stone Fruit

Whether you are making this for a small group or a huge crowd, this dish just jaw-dropping. The brilliant colors of the salmon and fruit are beautiful, and the aroma is amazing. While the fruit may seem an unconventional pairing with the salmon, I think of the fruit as the acid component (much like lemons) to balance out the rich fatty salmon. I also love the sweet, tart and spicy combination of the mustard and apricot preserves.

SERVES 4 TO 6
PREP TIME: 10 MINUTES
COOK TIME: 35 MINUTES

APRICOT MUSTARD GLAZE

1 tablespoon butter

1 shallot, finely minced

2 garlic cloves, finely minced

¼ cup white wine

¼ cup apricot jam
  or preserves

¼ cup spicy whole-grain
  mustard

kosher salt

1 wild salmon side
  (about 2 pounds)

kosher salt

2 peaches, cut in half,
  pits removed

2 nectarines, cut in half,
  pits removed

2 apricots, cut in half,
  pits removed

3 tablespoons butter

fresh chives or parsley
  leaves, for garnish

INGREDIENT NOTE: There are at least a dozen different types of salmon, each native to it's own region of the world. While they are all delicious, I try to buy the varieties that are local, and always spend the extra dollar for wild salmon.

1 First make the apricot-mustard glaze: Heat the butter in a small saucepan over medium heat until melted, but not browned. Add the shallot and garlic, sprinkle with salt and sweat the shallot over medium-low heat until soft and tender, 5 to 6 minutes. (Take care not to brown the shallots.)

2 Add the white wine and cook until most of the wine has evaporated, 2 to 3 minutes. Add the apricot jam and mustard and stir until well combined. As the jam starts to melt, continue to stir and cook for 3 to 4 minutes. Remove the sauce from the heat and set aside to cool.

3 Put the side of salmon, skin side down, on a large sheet of foil. Season the salmon generously with salt, and then spread half of the apricot-mustard glaze on the salmon. Set aside and reserve the extra sauce.

4 Place all of the fruit halves in a bowl. Melt the butter and pour it over the fruit. Toss the fruit in the butter to coat well.

5 Preheat the grill or a grill pan on medium heat.

6 Put the fruit on the grill, flat side down, and cook for 2 to 3 minutes. Return the fruit to the bowl and set aside.

7 Put the salmon, still on the sheet of foil, on the grill. Cook until the salmon is just cooked through but still bright pink in the center—depending on the thickness of the salmon, this should take between 7 and 10 minutes.

8 When the salmon is almost finished cooking, slather it with the rest of the glaze and let it melt into the fish.

9 When the fish is fully cooked, transfer it from the foil to a platter. Pile the grilled fruit into the corners of the platter, and garnish with the fresh chives or parsley.

Potato Salad with Mustard and Bacon

Potato salad is probably one of the most varied dishes around. I feel like every family has its own way of making it, and it is usually hard to stray from mom's recipe. Even I have deviated only slightly from my mom's version to create my own "Christo" variety, and now our little family has a standard recipe! Because I have a hate thing about mayonnaise (did I mention that already? I know, I can't stop talking about it), I make my dressing with whole-grain mustard, olive oil and red wine vinegar. I also like the crunchiness of celery, and the freshness of herbs mixed with the smoky bacon.

MAKE AHEAD: This salad could be made the day ahead, as it only gets more tasty as the flavors meld together and absorb into the potatoes. Just cover the bowl tightly with plastic wrap and refrigerate until ready to serve.

SERVES 4 TO 6
PREP TIME: 10 MINUTES
   (plus 1 to 24 hours for marinating)
COOK TIME: 35 MINUTES

kosher salt

2 pounds small red potatoes

3 strips thick-cut bacon

⅛ cup plus 1 teaspoon
   extra-virgin olive oil

½ small red onion, finely
   chopped

1 cloves garlic, minced

2 tablespoons whole-grain
   mustard

⅛ cup red wine vinegar

hot sauce

2 large stalks celery, finely
   chopped

½ cup chopped fresh
   mint leaves

½ cup chopped fresh parsley
   leaves

freshly ground black pepper

1 Bring a large pot of salted water to a boil. Add the potatoes and cook over medium heat for 20 minutes, or until fork-tender.

2 Meanwhile, cook the bacon in a skillet over medium heat until crispy. Set aside on a paper towel to drain and cool. Drain the extra fat out of the pan and discard, but keep the bacon-browned bits in the bottom of the pan.

3 Add 1 teaspoon of the olive oil to the pan along with the onion. Sprinkle with salt and cook until soft and lightly browned, about 5 minutes.

4 Transfer the onions to a large bowl. Add the garlic, mustard, vinegar, extra-virgin olive oil and a few shakes of hot sauce to the onions and whisk together. It should look like a salad dressing.

5 When the potatoes are tender, drain and let cool for a few minutes. Add the cooled potatoes to the dressing and toss, gently breaking up the potatoes with a spoon.

6 Crumble the bacon and add it to the potatoes with the celery, mint and parsley, gently tossing to combine. Season with salt and pepper. Cover with plastic wrap and refrigerate for up to one day, or until ready to serve.

Peach Cobbler

This is a very traditional cobbler. It is also exceptionally good. I know this because my sister Julie has made it several times every summer for the last few years, and she is very discriminating! I can assure you, if Julie loves it, you will love it too. Guaranteed. This cobbler is piled high with fresh summer peaches and a buttery sugary biscuit topping. It is best enjoyed with a scoop of vanilla ice cream or fresh whipped cream.

SERVES 8 TO 10
PREP TIME: 15 MINUTES
COOK TIME: 40 MINUTES

8 cups thinly sliced fresh peaches (about 8 peaches)

⅔ cup sugar

2 cups plus 3 tablespoons all-purpose flour

⅛ teaspoon nutmeg

½ cup (1 stick) unsalted butter, half cut into small pieces, half melted

¼ cup plus 6 tablespoons sugar

½ teaspoon salt

½ cup vegetable shortening

¼ cup ice water

pinch of cinnamon

vanilla ice cream or freshly whipped cream, for serving

INGREDIENT NOTE: This is a fantastic recipe for any time of year with any type of seasonal fresh fruit. My favorite variations are blackberry and pear cobblers.

1 Preheat the oven to 400°F. Prepare a 9x13x3-inch pan with baking spray or butter.

2 In a large bowl, mix the fruit with 3 tablespoons of the sugar, 3 tablespoons of the flour and the nutmeg. Gently toss to coat the fruit. Scatter the 4 tablespoons of butter pieces over the top of the fruit.

3 In a medium mixing bowl, put the remaining 2 cups flour, 3 tablespoons of sugar, the salt and the shortening. Cut the shortening into the dry ingredients with a pastry cutter or clean hands. Add the ice water and mix until you can squeeze the dough together to form a disc.

4 Break the dough up into smaller chunks and place them on top of the fruit. Drizzle the 4 tablespoons of melted butter over the dough, and then sprinkle with the remaining ¼ cup sugar mixed with the cinnamon.

5 Bake the cobbler for 40 minutes, until the pastry is golden brown and crispy and the fruit is bubbling. Serve with ice cream or whipped cream.

S'mores Cake

This is a perfect recipe, a wonderful play on the old-fashioned campfire combo of graham crackers, chocolate and toasted marshmallows. People freak out when they try this! It is spectacular in presentation, in taste, and in texture. It is a bit of an investment in time, but I promise it will be well worth it! If you want to bake this cake ahead of time, that is no problem. But the marshmallow topping should not be added until just before you are ready to serve. After a couple of hours it gets runny and soft—not quite as glamorous as when you serve it immediately.

GENEROUS TIPS: I cook the two graham cracker-chocolate cake layers with an "even cake layers" strip around them so that they turn out more flat. The third cake layer I leave alone because I want it to puff up and be domed for the top of the cake. These strips can be purchased at any kitchen store, and even in many grocery stores. If you can't find them, just smack the puffed up top down with a spatula right when the cake comes out of the oven. That usually gets the job done!

SERVES 10 TO 12
PREP TIME: 2 HOURS AND 30 MINUTES
COOK TIME: 45 MINUTES

DARK CHOCOLATE CAKE

1 cup dark unsweetened
   cocoa powder

2 cups boiling water

1 cup (2 sticks) unsalted butter, softened

2¼ cups sugar

1 tablespoon vanilla extract

4 large eggs

2¾ cups all-purpose flour

2 teaspoons baking soda

½ teaspoon baking powder

½ teaspoon salt

CHOCOLATE FUDGE FROSTING

1 pound semi-sweet chocolate pieces

2 cups heavy cream

BROWN BUTTER GRAHAM CRACKER CRUST

¾ cup (1½ sticks) unsalted butter

8 graham crackers (the whole rectangle)

½ cup sugar

½ teaspoon salt

MARSHMALLOW TOPPING

3 egg whites, at room temperature

¼ teaspoon salt

⅓ cup sugar

1 cup light corn syrup

2 tablespoons water

1 tablespoon vanilla bean paste

1 First make the frosting: Place the chocolate pieces in a medium heat-proof bowl. In a small pot, bring the cream to a simmer. Pour the cream over the chocolate pieces and let sit for about 5 minutes. Whisk the chocolate and cream until smooth and shiny. Set aside to cool and thicken (this can take up to an hour).

2 Preheat the oven to 350°F. Prepare three 8-inch round cake pans with circles of parchment paper and baking spray.

3 Make the graham cracker crust: Melt the butter and cook over low heat until golden brown, 5 to 7 minutes.

4 In a food processor, pulse the graham crackers with the sugar and salt until really fine. Transfer the crumbs to a medium bowl. Pour the brown butter over the crumbs and gently mix together until uniform moist crumbs form. Divide the graham cracker crumbs evenly between two of the three prepared pans, pressing them down firmly with a spatula. Set aside.

5 Next make the dark chocolate cake: Put the cocoa powder in a small bowl, and pour the boiling water on top of it. Whisk the water and cocoa together until smooth, and then set aside until cooled.

6 In a mixing bowl or standing mixer, beat the butter and sugar together until pale and fluffy. Add the vanilla and the eggs, one at a time, until well combined.

7 In a separate bowl, mix all of the dry ingredients together. Add half of the dry ingredients and half of the cooled liquid cocoa to the batter. Mix to combine. Repeat with the remaining half of the dry ingredients and the remaining half of the liquid cocoa; mix into a smooth batter. Divide the batter evenly among the three prepared pans. Gently spread the batter over the graham cracker crust in two of the pans. Bake for 25 minutes, taking care not to overbake the cakes.

8 Cool the cake layers in their pans on wire racks.

9 Cover a cake plate with a few strips of parchment or wax paper. Turn out one of the cake layers with the graham crust onto the prepared cake plate, graham layer up. Put a large dollop of fudge frosting on top of the crust and spread evenly onto the round. Follow with the second layer of cake with graham crust and another layer of fudge frosting. Finally, top with the third round, which is just cake, domed side up. Refrigerate the cake for at least 30 minutes, or up to 1 hour.

10 Meanwhile, make the marshmallow topping: In the bowl of a standing mixer, whisk the eggs and salt until pale and frothy.

11 Meanwhile, in a small pan, heat the sugar, corn syrup, water and vanilla bean paste over medium heat until the sugar has dissolved and the mixture has just reached a simmer, about 5 minutes.

12 With the mixer on medium speed, add a tiny bit of the hot sugar mixture to the egg whites. You want to temper the eggs, not scramble them! Keep adding a small amount at a time until eventually all of the sugar mixture has been added. Turn the mixer up to high speed and beat the topping for about 5 minutes, or until very stiff and shiny.

13 Remove the cake from the refrigerator. With the remaining fudge frosting, which should be stiff and glossy, frost the top and sides of the cake in a smooth even layer. Then carefully remove the parchment from the bottom of the cake to reveal a nice clean cake plate.

14 Mound the marshmallow frosting on top of the cake. (It should be stiff enough that it will stay put.) Using a kitchen torch, lightly toast the marshmallow frosting. Serve immediately.

CHAPTER THREE

Autumn

For our family, autumn means back to school for the kids, harvesting our garden's pumpkins and Brussels sprouts as well as the apples and pears from our own fruit trees. There is Halloween preparation, nature walks with the children to collect red and orange leaves, and the beginning of our hibernating weather. Comfort food abounds and baking with the girls on the kitchen counter with the dog at my feet becomes my favorite afternoon pastime. Entertaining in more intimate and cozy ways is my signature autumnal style.

AUTUMN MENUS

Sunday Dinner

MENU

- BRUSSELS SPROUTS
  WITH BACON AND LEEKS

- GREEK CHICKEN AND POTATOES

- APPLE AND CRANBERRY
  CROSTATA

Sunday dinner is one of those traditions that runs deep in my family. For years and years, my siblings and I gathered together at my parents' house for Sunday dinners—full of laughing, drinking and savoring my mom's cooking.

Now, we all have our own children and our lives have grown very busy, but we still make the effort to get everyone together frequently. The only real change is that now it is our children running and laughing through the old house where we grew up instead of us.

I try to keep this tradition alive in my own house as well. It's an evening of quiet and reconnection before work and school start the following morning. Everyone sits down together to talk and catch up with one another, and as with almost all other parts of my life, I like to do this over food.

Naturally, I am drawn to comforting dishes, regardless of the time of year, and the recipes I have included here are among my fall favorites. The smells of roasting chicken and baking apples fill our entire house, and before I know it, they lure the whole family right where I like them—to my kitchen table.

Brussels Sprouts with Bacon and Leeks

To me, these lovely little sprouts are like candy. Yes, I know we are talking about Brussels sprouts and, yes, I appreciate that this seems like a stretch! But truly, these Brussels sprouts come out tender and bright in flavor, and are deliciously studded with little bits of salty bacon and gorgeous swirls of yellow lemon zest. The fact that they are fast and easy to make means they have become one of my favorite fall staples. This dish pairs beautifully with any protein, and I even serve it tossed with fresh pasta.

SERVES 4 TO 6
PREP TIME: 5 MINUTES
COOK TIME: 20 MINUTES

2 pounds Brussels sprouts

6 slices thick-cut bacon, diced

2 medium leeks,
   white parts only, thinly
   sliced

2 cups chicken stock

zest of 2 lemons

kosher salt

1 Slice the Brussels sprouts in half and set aside.

2 In a large sauté pan over medium heat, cook the bacon until crispy and all of the fat has rendered, 5 to 7 minutes.

3 Add the leeks and cook another 2 to 3 minutes until the leeks are browned and soft. Add the Brussels sprouts, and stir to coat them with the bacon and leeks. Add the chicken stock and bring to a simmer. Add the lemon zest, cover the pan, and cook for 3 minutes.

4 Remove the cover and simmer until the chicken stock has cooked off, about 2 minutes. The sprouts should be tender (not mushy!). Season with kosher salt and serve hot.

Greek Chicken and Potatoes

If I had to choose my last meal, there is a definite chance that this would be it. This recipe comes from my mother-in-law, Tula. There is something so special about this chicken and potato dish that it is hard to describe without becoming very sentimental: Is is a meal that Tula made for me when I was getting back on my feet after the birth of each of my daughters. No one could deny that it is deeply comforting.

GENEROUS TIPS: The ingredients in this dish, while common, produce the most intense flavors. I had tried to imitate this chicken before, but it wasn't until I finally watched Tula prepare it that I understood what gives it its unique flavor— the quantity of the seasonings was boggling. The garlic in particular—eleven cloves is serious! However, because the chicken is slow roasted at a medium temperature for so long, the garlic winds up tasting nutty and even a little sweet. But it is the sourness of the lemon in combination with the roasted garlic pieces that creates the magic. The crazy amount of olive oil that crisps up the chicken and potatoes doesn't hurt either.

SERVES 4 TO 6
PREP TIME: 15 MINUTES
COOK TIME: 1 HOUR 15 MINUTES

1 whole chicken

2 lemons, plus wedges
   for garnish

⅔ cup olive oil

kosher salt and freshly
   ground black pepper

2 tablespoons dried oregano

11 garlic cloves, minced

8 medium white potatoes,
   peeled and quartered

1 Preheat the oven to 350°F.

2 Trim off the tips of the chicken wings and any extra fat.

3 Squeeze the juice of one lemon onto the chicken, and rub it into the front and back of the chicken halves. Pour ¼ cup of the olive oil over the chicken and rub again so that the skin is evenly coated. Generously season the chicken with salt and pepper and 1 tablespoon of the oregano. Sprinkle about half of the garlic over the chicken.

4 Place the potatoes in a large bowl. Add the remaining olive oil and garlic, remaining 1 tablespoon oregano, and the juice of 1 lemon. Season generously with salt and pepper and toss the potatoes until well coated with all the ingredients.

5 Arrange the potatoes on the sheet pan around the chicken. Pour any remaining liquid in the bowl on top. Roast the chicken and potatoes for about 1 hour and 15 minutes, or until both are golden and crispy.

6 Serve the chicken and potatoes with any extra sauce from the pan poured over them and fresh lemon wedges on the side. (Be sure to scrape up all the browned bits from the pan along with the sauce—those are the very best parts!)

Apple and Cranberry Crostata

A crostata is a casual alternative to baking an apple pie. It is much less precise and, really, I just call it "rustic" so I don't worry about how it looks as I throw it into the oven. As the crostata bakes, the smell of the apples, cranberries, cinnamon and ginger are completely intoxicating. And when this golden beauty comes out of the oven in all of its rustic glory, you will forget that you sort of just threw it together. Humble, fragrant and delicious, this is best served hot with a scoop of vanilla ice cream.

GENEROUS TIPS: The golden rule of a good pastry crust is handling the dough as little as possible. Don't overmix, it is okay if the dough is crumbly, as long as you can get it to press together when you remove it from the food processor. Roll the dough out between sheets of wax paper. This will keep it from getting toughened by excessive handling and from the flour that would be necessary to keep it from sticking.

MAKE AHEAD: The ginger pastry crust recipes makes 2 crusts; you can freeze them for up to 3 months.

SERVES 8 TO 10
PREP TIME: 15 MINUTES
  (plus 1 hour refrigeration time)
COOK TIME: 30 MINUTES

1 recipe Ginger Pastry Crust
  (see below)

6 cups peeled and thinly
  sliced sour apples

2 cups cranberries

1 tablespoon
  all-purpose flour

½ cup sugar, plus
  2 teaspoons for sprinkling

½ teaspoon ground ginger

½ teaspoon cinnamon

2 tablespoons
  unsalted butter

GINGER PASTRY CRUST

2¼ cups all-purpose flour

2 tablespoons sugar

1 teaspoon ground ginger

½ teaspoon kosher salt

½ cup (1 stick) cold unsalted
  butter, cut into pieces

½ cup vegetable shortening

⅓ cup ice-cold water

1 First make the ginger pastry crust: In the bowl of a food processor, place the flour, ½ cup sugar, the ginger and salt, then pulse to combine. Add the butter and vegetable shortening and pulse until the dough resembles coarse crumbs.

2 Add the ice-cold water a little at a time, and pulse until the dough comes together (you might not need all the water).

3 Form the dough into a disc and wrap it in wax paper. Refrigerate for at least 1 hour.

4 Preheat the oven to 400°F.

5 In a large bowl, combine the apples, cranberries, flour, sugar, ginger and cinnamon and toss gently together. Set aside.

6 Spread out a sheet of wax paper on the counter. Place the dough disc in the middle, and place another sheet of wax paper over the top. Roll the dough out into a large oval. The dough should be about ¼ inch thick. It does not need to be perfect!

7 Pour the apple and cranberry mixture into the center of the dough and then gently fold the sides of the dough in toward the center to hold the filling in while the crostata bakes. Dot the top of the fruit with pieces of the butter and sprinkle the edges of the dough with the remaining 2 teaspoons sugar. Bake the crostata for 30 minutes, or until the crust is golden brown and the fruit is bubbling.

8 Serve immediately or at room temperature.

PASTRY CRUST VARIATIONS: If I am going to the trouble to make pastry crust, I usually make several batches to freeze. You can make this basic recipe, or create any number of variations. Add fresh herbs like rosemary, thyme or dried oregano for a savory tart or a pot-pie crust. Dried spices such as cinnamon or nutmeg lend a depth of flavor to sweet pastry crust. To store, just split the finished dough into two discs and wrap really well in plastic wrap. Label and date them and place in the freezer for a rainy day, it will keep up to 3 months.

Halloween Supper

MENU

- MACARONI AND CHEESE WITH PUMPKIN AND BACON

- SPICY ARUGULA WITH CANDIED PECANS AND BALSAMIC DRESSING

- PECAN CARAMEL COCONUT BARS

- PUMPKIN GINGERSNAP TRIFLE

Anyone who knows me knows that Halloween is high on my list of favorite days. I relish the decorations, the treats and above all else—the costumes! I have been known to spend weeks creating homemade costumes for my nieces and nephews, and now for my own children. I never take these things lightly, and will spend hours at a stretch intensely sewing on feathers and hot glue-gunning accessories. Decorating the house is almost as much fun; see Glitter Decorations, opposite, for my over-the-top tips. (Nobody said I was normal.)

On Halloween night, some of our closest friends gather at our home for pre-trick-or-treating nourishment. I always try to choose dishes that both the children and the adults will be excited about, so that the kids are sure to fill their little bellies with something besides chocolate. This year it was macaroni and cheese, fittingly served in a pumpkin.

I added the green salad for the sake of the grownups, as well as the desserts, which we munch on long after the children are busy running through the neighborhood. One of my favorite parts of the night? When the dads have taken the children out for trick-or-treating and the ladies can catch up over a glass of wine while waiting for trick-or-treaters to ring the doorbell. A rare treat for any mother!

GLITTER DECORATIONS

I have a weakness for all things sparkly. Perhaps even specifically for glitter. Halloween is as a good a time as any to really indulge in all things crafty, and decorating the house is no exception. The style I most enjoy for this holiday is what I have dubbed "creepy glamour." Maybe that term leaves some creativity to be desired, but I think it gets the point across: Scary, but stylish.

I scour craft stores, dollar stores and even my own basement looking simply for things that would ordinarily be considered creepy. I gather everything from Styrofoam bones to cheap plastic spider rings. Then I brush them with craft glue and dunk them liberally in glitter. It is that easy. The style comes in with the color of the glitter that you use and how they are displayed. I am partial to silver and black glitter, but green and purple are spectacular as well. And, as with all displays, there is strength in numbers.

Macaroni and Cheese with Pumpkin and Bacon

Pete and I have become famous for our macaroni and cheese, amongst our friends, at least. I'm not really sure that there is any dish more comforting and consistently sure to produce huge smiles. For me, playing with the mac and cheese ingredients to suit each season and occasion is part of the fun—the other, much larger part, is eating it, of course! So, whether it is by changing up the cheeses and adding lobster, as in Lobster Macaroni and Cheese (page 194), or by adding pumpkin and bacon as I have done here, this dish can take on many personalities.

GENEROUS TIP: I have upped the ante baking this recipe in a pumpkin. While it is indeed a showstopper (and very easy for the fantastic results), this mac and cheese will be just as celebrated if you serve it in a humble baking dish.

SERVES 6 TO 8
PREP TIME: 10 MINUTES
COOK TIME: 1 HOUR 15 MINUTES

One 8-pound pumpkin, preferably the Cinderella variety (optional)

kosher salt and freshly ground black pepper

1 pound macaroni noodles

6 strips thick-cut bacon

½ cup (1 stick) unsalted butter

1 large yellow onion, finely chopped

2 cups pumpkin, diced (squash would also be delicious)

¼ cup all-purpose flour

2 cups heavy cream

1 cup whole milk

1 clove garlic, minced

4 cups shredded sharp Cheddar cheese

¼ to ½ teaspoon cayenne pepper

1 Preheat the oven to 375°F. If you are not using the pumpkin, prepare a 9 x 13 x 2-inch baking dish with cooking spray.

2 If using the pumpkin, slice off the top one-third of the way down. Scrape out and discard the seeds and pulp to create a bowl. Generously salt and pepper the inside of the pumpkin.

3 Place the pumpkin and its top directly on a baking stone or on a large sheet pan and bake for 1 hour, or until tender.

4 Meanwhile, make the macaroni: Bring a large pot of salted water to a boil. Add the macaroni noodles and boil until 1 minute shy of their al dente cooking time, according to the package instructions. Drain, rinse with cool water, drain again and set aside.

5 Cook the bacon in a large heavy pot over medium heat until crispy and all the fat has been rendered, 5 to 7 minutes. Drain the bacon, chop roughly and set aside.

6 In the same pot over medium heat, melt ¼ cup of the butter into the bacon fat. Add the onion and cook until soft, 4 to 5 minutes. Add the pumpkin cubes and cook for 6 to 8 minutes—the pumpkin should be just tender, not mushy or falling apart. Season with salt, transfer to a medium bowl and set aside.

7 In the same heavy pot over medium heat, melt the remaining ¼ cup butter. Add the flour and cook for 2 to 3 minutes, stirring constantly with a wooden spoon, until the butter and flour form a smooth paste or roux. Add the cream, 1 cup at a time, stirring constantly. Add the milk and stir the roux until smooth. Stir in the garlic. Add the cheese and stir until very smooth. Add the cayenne pepper and season with salt.

8 Remove the sauce from the heat and add the macaroni noodles. Add the onions, pumpkin and bacon and stir everything together really well. Spoon the macaroni into the pumpkin (or the baking dish) and bake for 30 minutes, until the macaroni and cheese is very hot and bubbly on the edges and the top is crispy and golden.

9 Serve immediately.

Spicy Arugula with Candied Pecans and Balsamic Dressing

Dark, peppery greens dressed in a classic balsamic dressing are like the little black dress of salads in my opinion. This salad could be coaxed in many directions with simple substitutions of different fruit (dried or fresh) and any type of cheese or nuts you could dream of. For the fall season, I've included juicy ripe pear, crispy candied pecans and creamy Gorgonzola cheese. As soon as you introduce this into your salad repertoire, it will be in your rotation permanently!

MAKE AHEAD: Both the candied pecans and balsamic dressing can be made days ahead of time.

SERVES 4 TO 6
PREP TIME: 5 MINUTES
COOK TIME: 10 MINUTES

CANDIED PECANS

1 egg white

1 teaspoon plus
   a pinch of kosher salt

2 cups pecans

1 cup sugar

½ teaspoon cinnamon

⅛ teaspoon cayenne pepper

BALSAMIC DRESSING

2 small garlic cloves

2 tablespoons Dijon mustard

1 tablespoon brown sugar

3 dashes of
   Worcestershire sauce

⅓ cup balsamic vinegar

½ cup extra-virgin olive oil

2 tablespoons water

kosher salt and freshly
   ground black pepper

8 cups arugula or mixed
   greens

1 ripe pear, thinly sliced

4 ounces Gorgonzola cheese,
   crumbled

1. First make the candied pecans: Preheat the oven to 350°F. Prepare a sheet pan with a silpat liner or parchment paper.

2. In a medium bowl, whisk the egg white with a pinch of salt until frothy and pale. Add the nuts and gently toss to coat. Add ½ cup of the sugar and toss. Add the remaining ½ cup sugar, 1 teaspoon salt and the cinnamon and cayenne pepper. Toss to coat and spread the nuts on the prepared sheet pan. Bake for 10 minutes.

3. Remove the nuts from the oven and stir them around with a spatula. Bake for an additional 5 minutes.

4. Remove the nuts from the oven, stir them once more and let cool. Store in an airtight container in the pantry for up to 2 months, or until ready to use.

5. Next make the balsamic dressing: Put all the ingredients except the salt and pepper into a blender and blend on low until thick and well combined. The dressing will take on a pale brown color and a creamy consistency. Season with salt and pepper. Refrigerate for up to 5 days, or until ready to use.

6. In a serving bowl, toss the arugula with the balsamic dressing. Top the salad with the pear slices, crumbled Gorgonzola and the candied pecans.

Pecan Caramel Coconut Bars

I have always had a thing for pecan pie. Gooey, buttery, brown sugary—what's not to love? But take all that and slap it onto a coconut shortbread crust to create a snack-sized treat—well, that's a thing of beauty. These insanely good pecan bars have long been a favorite of mine. They are perfect for a dessert buffet, or even just a decadent afterschool snack! Frankly, I would even eat them for breakfast.

MAKES 24 BARS
PREP TIME: 5 MINUTES
COOK TIME: 35 MINUTES

2 cups pecans

COCONUT SHORTBREAD CRUST

2 cups all-purpose flour

1 cup powdered sugar

1 cup shredded unsweetened coconut

½ teaspoon salt

1 cup (2 sticks) cold unsalted butter, cut into small pieces

PECAN FILLING

10 tablespoons (1¼ sticks) unsalted butter

1½ cups brown sugar

½ cup heavy cream

1 teaspoon vanilla extract

1 teaspoon salt

INGREDIENT NOTE: If you are not a coconut lover, just omit the coconut. The crust will still turn out perfectly without it.

1   Preheat the oven to 350ºF.

2   Pour the pecans out onto a sheet pan and toast in the oven for 7 minutes. Set aside.

3   Make the coconut shortbread crust: Pulse together the flour, sugar, coconut, and salt in the bowl of a food processor. Add the cold butter and pulse until a coarse crumb forms.

4   Transfer the shortbread crust dough into a 9 x 13 x 2-inch baking pan. Use the bottom off a measuring cup to pack the crust down tightly.

5   Make the pecan filling: In a medium saucepan over medium heat, melt the butter. Add the brown sugar, cream, vanilla and salt and whisk together until smooth. Cook for 2 to 3 minutes, or until gently bubbling.

6   Sprinkle the reserved pecans over the crust. Pour the filling over the pecans, tilting the baking pan around so that the filling evenly spreads over the crust. Bake the bars for 25 minutes. Remove from the oven and let cool completely in the pan before cutting.

7   To cut the bars, run a knife around the edges of the pan. Slice the bars into 24 squares and remove with a spatula.

Pumpkin Gingersnap Trifle

Tender layers of sweet pumpkin cake alternate with crispy, crunchy, spicy gingersnap crumbs and soft peaks of whipped cream in this autumnal trifle, which always makes an annual appearance on my father's birthday as it's his favorite. Trifle is a hostess's dream, as it really tastes best a day after it is made, so you have to do nothing but pull it out of the refrigerator and serve once dessert time rolls around.

MAKE AHEAD: This dessert can—and should—be made and refrigerated a day before serving.

SERVES 10 TO 12
PREP TIME: 30 MINUTES
COOK TIME: 30 MINUTES

PUMPKIN CAKE

¾ cup (1½ sticks) unsalted butter, at room temperature

1½ cups sugar

1½ teaspoons vanilla extract

3 large eggs

1¼ cups pumpkin puree

3 cups all-purpose flour

1 teaspoons baking powder

1 teaspoons baking soda

½ teaspoon salt

2 teaspoons cinnamon

½ teaspoons ground nutmeg

½ teaspoons ground ginger

1 cup buttermilk

GINGERSNAP CRUMBLE

3 cups gingersnap cookies

¼ teaspoon salt

2 tablespoons unsalted butter, melted

2 tablespoons sugar

MAPLE WHIPPED CREAM

2 cups heavy cream, chilled

2 tablespoons powdered sugar

2 teaspoons maple extract

1 Preheat the oven to 325°F. Prepare two 9-inch round cake pans with baking spray.

2 Make the pumpkin cake: In the bowl of a standing mixer, beat the butter and sugar together over medium speed until light and fluffy, about 2 minutes. Add the vanilla and eggs and beat over medium speed to combine. Add the pumpkin puree and beat until well combined. It will look like the batter has curdled, but it is fine!

3 In a separate bowl, sift together the flour, baking powder and soda, salt, cinnamon, nutmeg and ginger. Add half of the flour mixture to the batter, and then ½ cup of the buttermilk. Combine completely over low speed. Add the rest of the flour mixture and the remaining ½ cup buttermilk and mix until completely combined.

4 Divide the batter evenly between the two cake pans and bake for 25 to 30 minutes, or until a toothpick inserted in the center comes out clean. Remove the cakes from the heat and let them cool completely on a rack.

5 Meanwhile, make the gingersnap crumble: In the bowl of a food processor, pulse the gingersnaps and salt until a fine crumb forms. With the machine still running, pour in the melted butter and process until the crumb is moist and uniform. Set aside.

6 Finally, make the maple whipped cream: Pour the cold heavy cream into a large bowl. With an electric mixer, whip the cream until soft peaks form, about 3 minutes. Add the powdered sugar and the maple extract and whip until slightly thickened and well combined.

7 To assemble the trifle, slice each cake round into 6 wedges or 12 total. Push 4 of the layers into the bottom of a trifle dish (it is okay if you have to kind of smash them in there). Spoon a third of the maple whipped cream over the top of the cake and then sprinkle a third of the gingersnap crumble over the whipped cream. Repeat this twice to create three layers of trifle topped with cream and gingersnap crumble.

8 Refrigerate at least 2 hours and up to 1 day before serving. Serve by spooning the chilled trifle into bowls.

Girls' Night

MENU

- BLENDED POMEGRANATE MARGARITAS

- GUACAMOLE

- BUTTERNUT SQUASH ENCHILADAS WITH SALSA VERDE AND CILANTRO LIME CRÈME

- GREEN SALAD WITH CORN, PEPPERS AND SMOKY RED PEPPER DRESSING

- ICE CREAM SUNDAES WITH TEQUILA CARAMEL SAUCE

If you are anything like me, once you are married, and especially if you have children, you will come to appreciate the mighty power of a girls' night. It is more than the fact that you are refilling wineglasses instead of sippy cups, it is a chance to shave fun with your girlfriends without worrying about your partner or child. For me, girls' night is a mini-vacation, a time to drink and eat and laugh uninterrupted. Remind me to schedule these more often!

When it is my turn to host, I really want to be able to enjoy myself while treating my tired, weary friends to a special night. For this particular girls' night, I went with Mexican food, which is always popular and easy to prepare ahead of time. Every element can be made earlier in the day, leaving only the baking of the enchiladas and the blending of the margaritas when your friends arrive. This also happens to be a vegetarian meal, something that is far more difficult to get away with when the gentleman in my life are around, but appreciated by the women.

I dress the table with bright colors and easy flower arrangements as well as basic white platters and plates. The contrast gives everything a clean and festive feel, and is as easy to create as the guacamole!

SIMPLE FLOWER ARRANGING

I love to create my own flower arrangements, but I am by no means a florist. So, I employ these simple tricks to keep my arrangements economical and looking professional.

• Choose just one type and color of flower. Roses, tulips, peonies, carnations—whatever you pick, it is hard to go wrong if you are using just one type and color.

• Keep the arrangements low and tight. If the blooms are tightly packed and low to the top of the vessel, you will avoid the challenge of complicated varying heights.

• If you really want to use more than one type of flower, choose blossoms that are all the same color, or choose the same type of flower, but in multiple shades. But again, remember to keep it low and tight in the vases.

• If you are comfortable with the above tips, then consider sprucing up your arrangement with unexpected touches. Fresh mint, sprigs of thyme or golden oregano, or fresh fruit are all easy and inventive ways to dress up your blooms.

• Don't be afraid of filler flowers. Baby's Breath, carnations, ragweed, daisies—they are as gorgeous as any rose when bundled in large quantities; just keep them low and tight!

Blended Pomegranate Margaritas

This is a festive blend of traditional margarita flavors with sweet and bitter pomegranate juice. I find it the best possible combination for this slushy treat, and the fact that it is a lovely shade of pink for a "girls' night" doesn't hurt either!

SERVES 2
PREP TIME: 5 MINUTES

2 cups ice cubes

½ cup pomegranate juice

¼ cup fresh lime juice

¼ cup tequila

⅛ cup triple sec

1 tablespoon sugar

pomegranate seeds and
  lime wedges, for garnish

1   Pour all of the ingredients into a blender and blend on high speed until frothy and slushy and all of the ice cubes are blended, about 30 seconds.

2   Pour into chilled margarita glasses and garnish each with fresh pomegranate seeds and a lime wedge.

3   Serve immediately.

Guacamole

Guacamole was sent from heaven as far as I am concerned. Dip it, spread it, eat it by the spoonful—it doesn't really matter to me as long as there is a big bowl with plenty of fresh lime and salt.

SERVES 4 TO 6
PREP TIME: 10 MINUTES

½ cup minced white onion

1 jalapeño pepper, minced

2 tablespoons fresh cilantro,
  leaves and stems,
  finely chopped

6 ripe avocados, peeled
  and pits removed

2 limes

kosher salt

1   In a medium bowl, combine the onion, jalapeño and cilantro.

2   Add the avocado in large chunks, and mash the ingredients together with a fork.

3   Add the juice of 1 lime. Taste and adjust the seasoning with the other lime and the kosher salt.

Butternut Squash Enchiladas

These enchiladas combine some of my favorites things—butternut squash, goat cheese and salsa verde—and harmoniously blend them together into little packages of perfection. These are completely non-traditional enchiladas, which is partly why I love them so much. It is a new (and vegetarian!) take on an old favorite that has ended up being a highly requested dish amongst the ladies in my life.

MAKE AHEAD: Roast and puree the squash a day ahead; just refrigerate in an airtight container.

SERVES 4 TO 6
PREP TIME: 20 MINUTES
COOK TIME: 1 HOUR

1 butternut squash
   (about 1½ pounds)

1 tablespoon butter

kosher salt

¼ cup plus
   1 tablespoon
   vegetable oil

1 yellow onion,
   thinly sliced

12 corn tortillas

10 ounces soft
   goat cheese

2 cups shredded
   Monterey Jack cheese

SALSA VERDE
   (see opposite page)

CILANTRO LIME CRÈME
   (see opposite page)

1   Preheat the oven to 400°F.

2   Slice the butternut squash into quarters and scoop the seeds out of the center. Place the pieces of squash, skin side down, on a baking sheet and dot the butter over the squash. Sprinkle generously with salt and roast for about 30 minutes, until the squash is fork-tender.

3   Meanwhile, make the salsa verde.

4   When the squash is done roasting, let it cool until you can handle it. Pour the butter that has collected in the squash centers into the bowl of a food processor. Using a sharp knife, gently peel the skin off the pieces of squash and discard. Cut the flesh into chunks and add to the food processor. Puree the squash until smooth and creamy. Set aside.

5   Preheat the oven to 375°F. Prepare a 9 x 13 x 2-inch baking dish by spreading 1½ cups salsa verde over the bottom of the dish.

6   In a large sauté pan, heat 1 tablespoon of the vegetable oil over high. Add the onion slices and a sprinkle of salt. Fry the onions until they are golden brown, about 5 minutes. Transfer to a plate and set aside.

7   In the same pan, heat the remaining ¼ cup of vegetable oil over low heat. Using tongs, lightly sweep each tortilla through the hot vegetable oil, and then set the tortillas on a cutting board to prepare the enchiladas. The hot oil will make the tortillas soft and pliable so they don't break when they are rolled. (I like to work in batches of two tortillas at a time.)

8   In the center of each tortilla, add 2 tablespoons squash puree, some fried onions and a little less than an ounce of goat cheese. Roll the tortillas and place them side by side in the prepared baking dish: 12 enchiladas total or 2 rows of 6. Pour another 1½ cups of the salsa over the tops of the enchiladas. Spread it evenly, making sure to cover the edges of the tortillas. Sprinkle the Monterey Jack over the top of the enchiladas and bake for 20 minutes, until the enchiladas are piping hot, much of the salsa's liquid has been absorbed and the cheese is golden brown.

9   Serve immediately with the rest of the salsa verde and the cilantro lime crème on the side.

Salsa Verde

I am so in love with this multi-functional salsa. It's bright and fresh and full of flavor. There is nothing in this but raw vegetables and herbs (so it couldn't be healthier!) and it will delight you. Besides using it as a dip or sauce, it is also wonderful as a salad dressing or marinade for fish, chicken or pork.

MAKES 4 TO 5 CUPS
PREP TIME: 5 MINUTES

3 cups chopped green tomatoes
    (about 1½ pounds)

2 cups chopped tomatillos (8 to 10)

1 jalapeño pepper, chopped, most
    seeds removed (add another
    jalapeño if you like it spicy)

4 garlic cloves, peeled

½ yellow onion

½ cup roughly chopped fresh
    cilantro leaves and stems

kosher salt

Throw all of the ingredients except the salt in the bowl of a food processor and puree until smooth. Season to taste with salt. Refrigerate in an airtight container for up to 5 days.

Cilantro Lime Creme

This crème sauce is the first sour cream–based recipe that I really enjoyed. I could never bring myself to glop sour cream onto my food before, maybe it was just too white or too plain. But once it has been dressed up with fresh lime zest, garlic and fragrant cilantro, a dip of beauty that perfectly complements and cools any spicy dish. And, yes, I glop this crème on everything.

MAKES 1 CUP
PREP TIME: 2 MINUTES

8 ounces sour cream

2 tablespoons fresh cilantro,
    leaves and stems, finely minced

zest of 1 lime

1 tablespoon fresh lime juice

1 garlic clove, finely minced

kosher salt

Mix together all of the ingredients except the salt in a small bowl, then season generously with salt. Refrigerate in an airtight container for up to 3 days.

Green Salad with Corn, Peppers and Smoky Red Pepper Dressing

There is nothing like a really great salad, full of bright, fresh and zesty flavors, to tie the rest of a meal together. This one is dressed with an incredible Smoky Red Pepper Dressing that ensures you will be chomping at the bit for an extra serving!

MAKE AHEAD: The smoky red pepper dressing yields 1 cup; you can make it ahead and refrigerate any left over.

SERVES 4 TO 6
PREP TIME: 10 MINUTES

SMOKY RED PEPPER DRESSING

¼ cup olive oil

⅛ cup plus 1 tablespoon red wine vinegar

2 ounces roasted red peppers (packed in water and drained)

2 tablespoons fresh cilantro leaves

1 garlic clove, peeled

1 teaspoon smoked paprika

½ teaspoon salt

8 cups green lettuce, torn into bite-size pieces

1 cup fresh raw corn kernels

1 red bell pepper, small diced

1 yellow bell pepper, small diced

1 shallot, small diced

½ cup Smoky Red Pepper Dressing (see above)

1. First make the smoky red pepper dressing: In a blender, combine the olive oil, vinegar, roasted peppers, cilantro, garlic, paprika and salt. Puree until the dressing is completely smooth. Taste to adjust with salt. You will have about 1 cup. Pour into an airtight container and refrigerate for up to 5 days, or until needed.

2. In a large bowl, combine the lettuce, corn, red and yellow peppers and shallot and toss to combine. Add ½ cup of the dressing and gently toss everything to coat. Serve immediately.

Ice Cream Sundaes with Tequila Caramel Sauce

I am a sucker for caramel. I have suffered burns for it because I was too impatient to spoon it into my mouth, dribbling it all over my arm and chin. Shameful. And, frankly, I prefer a splash of ice cream with my caramel versus the other way around. Adding tequila was an interesting variation for me. Whiskey? Delicious. Bourbon? Of course! Turns out tequila is equally superb and a fantastic way to give these grownup ice cream sundaes a kick.

MAKE AHEAD: The tequila caramel sauce can be made weeks ahead.

SERVES 4 TO 6
PREP TIME: 2 MINUTES
COOK TIME: 10 MINUTES

TEQUILA CARAMEL SAUCE

1 cup sugar

¼ cup tequila

½ cup heavy cream

1 quart good-quality vanilla ice cream

1 cup chopped chocolate-covered cashews

1 In a sauté pan, melt the sugar over medium heat. When the sugar has turned an amber color, about 5 minutes, whisk in the tequila. Be careful: The tequila will light on fire if it sloshes near the flame! When the tequila is fully incorporated, whisk in the cream. The sugar will seize up, but just keep whisking until the sugar and cream have created a smooth sauce, 2 to 3 minutes. You will have about 1½ cups.

2 Let the caramel cool until warm before serving. It will thicken as it cools. The caramel can be kept in the refrigerator in an airtight container for up to 3 weeks. To reheat the sauce, warm it gently over low heat before serving.

3 To serve, divide the ice cream among serving bowls, and top with desired amounts of warm tequila caramel sauce and chocolate covered cashews. (I tend to use up the entire 1½ cups caramel sauce here.)

Game Night

MENU

- SPICY CHEESE BREADSTICKS

- STICKY ASIAN CHICKEN WINGS

- BLUE CHEESE DIP

- STEAK SANDWICHES WITH BRIE AND FIG SPREAD

- CHOCOLATE PEANUT BUTTER BROWNIES

Oh how I love a good game night! We gather all of our friends around the game table and play cards for hours and hours. As the night winds on, it gets progressively louder and I always wonder (with some delight) if everyone on the block can hear the shouting and laughing.

An integral part to the success of this evening is, of course, the food and drinks. For this party, I created gourmet versions of my favorite bar snacks, taking things like hot wings and chips and dip and making beautiful homemade renditions—familiar standbys, only done much, much better! I presented all of the food piled high on platters and in bowls on a central table, accompanied by appetizer plates so guests can graze or fill their plate as they take breaks from the typically intense card games.

For a game night, the spread should consist only of finger food. Nobody wants to fuss with knives and forks when they have cards to hold. And, don't forget, because it is finger food, make sure that you have lots of napkins available!

Finally, it would not be game night without the cocktails. I like to set out a self-serve bar with ice, garnishes, and a few of the liquors and mixers that my friends like. Plus I always make sure the fixings for a good dirty martini are on hand!

HOW TO SET UP A SELF-SERVE BAR

Place the bar where you want everyone to gather, as the bar will always attract the crowd. My alcoholic picks for a no-fail bar are at minimum: one white wine, one red wine, vodka, gin and Scotch. Make sure you have soda water, tonic and cranberry juice, as well as lemons, limes and green olives on hand, too. Twice as much ice as you think you will need is essential, as is a good supply of cocktail napkins and plenty of clean glasses.

You can build on a bar from there. Add beer, extra mixers for cocktails and, for a wild crowd, you can add tequila and rum. If your friends are more into drinking wine, then add an additional choice or two for the wines. A bubbly option is always appreciated.

Display everything nicely and check in on the bar often. While you don't have to position yourself as the bartender, make sure that there are no dirty glasses or wadded up napkins messing up your beautiful bar. Snacks or a small flower arrangement are always a nice touch. By combining store-bought potato chips with a homemade dip, and presenting them in an attractive way, chips and dip becomes a good-humored and elegant gourmet bar snack.

Spicy Cheese Breadsticks

This is a shortcut recipe that I use again and again. Besides being so tasty and convenient, these breadsticks make for a pretty presentation. I regularly stick these on the edge of the bar and guests are always impressed by them. They are so easy to make, that I kind of feel like I am cheating. I simply season raw puff pastry dough with spices and cheese, then slice and twist the dough. After baking, you are left with delicious, flakey, hot and buttery breadsticks with little bits of melting cheese. I love that I can flavor these any way I want depending on what I have in my spice pantry and cheese drawer.

MAKES 8 BREADSTICKS
PREP TIME: 5 MINUTES
COOK TIME: 15 MINUTES

1 sheet of puff pastry

flour, for rolling out
  the dough

1 tablespoon sesame seeds

1 tablespoon poppy seeds

1 teaspoon fennel seeds

1 teaspoon kosher salt

¼ teaspoon cayenne pepper

½ cup finely shredded
  Cheddar cheese

1 Preheat the oven to 400°F. Prepare a sheet pan with parchment paper or a silpat liner.

2 On a lightly floured surface, roll out the sheet of puff pastry dough until it is very thin.

3 In a small bowl, mix together the sesame, poppy and fennel seeds with the salt and cayenne and sprinkle them over the dough. Now evenly sprinkle the cheese over the dough and, using a rolling pin, press all of the toppings into the dough. Slice the dough into eight even strips. Twist each dough strip from both ends so that the dough spirals into a breadstick, tucking any thin ends under. They will not be perfect and that is okay, you just do not want them too thin in the center, or they may snap in half after baking.

4 Transfer the breadsticks to the prepared sheet pan and bake for 15 minutes, or until golden.

5 Let cool for a few minutes, then transfer the breadsticks to a tall glass and fan out to serve.

Sticky Asian Chicken Wings

My daughter Pia is obsessed with chicken wings. I'm not sure how this happened as I've never made them at home before, but so be it. In answer to her never-ending requests that I make her "favorite chicken wings," these sweet, spicy, sour, crispy, juicy Sticky Asian Chicken Wings were born. Warning: These are so irresistible you may find yourself hovering over the bowl at the kitchen counter, smacking your lips and licking your fingers and hoping that no one walks in and sees you eating like a wild animal. That is how good these are. Guess what? Now I am obsessed with chicken wings, too.

SERVES 4 TO 6
PREP TIME: 15 MINUTES
COOK TIME: 15 MINUTES

2½ pounds chicken wings with tips

2 cups all-purpose flour

2 teaspoons kosher salt

vegetable oil, for frying

3 tablespoons rice wine vinegar

2 tablespoons red wine vinegar

2 tablespoons hoisin sauce

2 tablespoons honey

2 tablespoons fresh ginger, peeled and chopped

2 cloves garlic

1 tablespoon brown sugar

2 teaspoons soy sauce

2 teaspoons siracha sauce (add more if you want them really spicy)

1 teaspoon cornstarch

2 tablespoons butter

thinly sliced green onions and toasted sesame seeds, for garnish

1   Rinse the chicken wings with cold water and drain.

2   Combine the flour and salt in a large baking dish.

3   Add several inches of vegetable oil to a large heavy pot. Heat the oil over medium heat until a candy or deep-frying thermometer registers 375°F.

4   Meanwhile, add the chicken wings to the flour mixture and toss to coat lightly. (You will probably have to do this in two batches; same with the frying.)

5   Gently add the chicken wings to the oil. Fry, stirring and flipping the wings occasionally, for about 12 minutes or until golden. Make sure you keep an eye on the heat so that it stays a consistent 375°F. Transfer the chicken wings directly to a large bowl.

6   Meanwhile, make the sauce. In a small bowl, whisk together the rice and red wine vinegars, hoisin and honey.

7   Run the garlic and ginger through a garlic press to get rid of fibrous material. (If you don't have one, then finely mince the garlic and ginger.) Add to the bowl along with the brown sugar, soy sauce and siracha and combine well. Whisk in the cornstarch.

8   Melt the butter in a saucepan over medium heat. Whisk in the sauce and cook for about 1 minute to allow the cornstarch to thicken the sauce.

9   Add half of the sauce to the first batch of wings and toss to coat. Sprinkle with green onions and sesame seeds.

10 Repeat with the second batch of chicken wings, sauce and garnish. Serve immediately.

Blue Cheese Dip

My husband absolutely loves blue cheese dip. In fact, it's one of the few ways I can get him to eat his veggies. Me? Not so much. But I can't deprive him, so I worked hard to concoct my own dip—one that I would feel good about serving to our friends and eating myself. This version uses cottage cheese as the base, leaving a creamy blank canvas for the blue cheese and fresh herbs to shine. I added some fresh lemon juice to balance the strong flavors in the dip. This works really well as a sandwich spread as well.

MAKE AHEAD: This dip can be made up to 5 days before serving; just refrigerate in an airtight container.

MAKES 2¼ CUPS
PREP TIME: 5 MINUTES

2 cups cottage cheese

4 ounces blue cheese

2 cloves garlic, minced

1 tablespoon fresh
   lemon juice

2 tablespoons minced
   fresh chives

kosher salt and freshly
   ground black pepper

In the bowl of a food processor or in a blender, combine the cottage cheese, blue cheese, garlic and lemon juice. Puree until the dip is quite smooth. Add the chives and pulse until just combined. Season with salt and pepper. Transfer the dip to a serving bowl and serve immediately, or cover with plastic wrap and refrigerate until needed.

Balsamic Onions

Sweet, savory and tart, this syrupy onion concoction adds incredible dimension to any sandwich. I love these as a way to dress up a basic grilled cheese.

MAKE AHEAD: This can be made ahead and kept in an airtight container for up to a week in the fridge.

MAKES 1½ CUPS
PREP TIME: 2 MINUTES
COOK TIME: 50 MINUTES

2 tablespoons unsalted butter

2 yellow onions, thinly sliced
   against the grain

kosher salt

2 cups water

1 sprig fresh thyme

1 tablespoon sugar

2 tablespoons balsamic vinegar

1 In a sauté pan over medium heat, melt the butter. Add the onions and sprinkle with salt. Cook until softened and slightly browned, about 5 minutes.

2 Add 1 cup of the water and cook the onions, stirring often, until the water evaporates, about 20 minutes.

3 Add the remaining cup water and the thyme. Cook until the onions are very soft, and the liquid has all been cooked off, another 20 minutes. Sprinkle the onions with the sugar and balsamic vinegar. Mix thoroughly and simmer another 5 minutes.

4 Season with salt. Discard the thyme sprig and refrigerate until ready to use.

Steak Sandwiches with Brie and Fig Spread

This is the ultimate steak sandwich. It satisfies our carnivorous, red-meat happy friends while the addition of sweet fig and tangy Balsamic Onions delights the ladies. My husband is especially pleased to see that I don't even feel the need to add any greens. The truth is, this sandwich doesn't need it. It is all about embracing the flavor of the steak, and letting it melt in your mouth on a velvety pillow of brie cheese. Enough said.

**MAKES 6 SANDWICHES
PREP TIME: 20 MINUTES**
   (including resting time)
COOK TIME: 10 MINUTES

2 pounds boneless
   rib eye
   (about 2 steaks)

2 teaspoons
   vegetable oil

kosher salt and freshly
   ground black pepper

6 soft French rolls
   (about 8 inches long)

¾ cup fig spread

1 pound Brie,
   at room temperature

1½ cups Balsamic Onions
   (see page 145)

1   Place a cast-iron skillet or ovenproof pan in the oven and preheat the oven to 500°F. Bring the steaks to room temperature. Drizzle them with the vegetable oil and rub it in on all sides. Generously season the steaks with salt and pepper.

2   When the oven reaches 500°F, pull the pan out and place on the stovetop over high heat. Sear the steaks in the pan for 2 minutes on one side, then flip and cook another 2 minutes on the other side. Return the pan to the oven and cook the steaks, about 4 minutes for medium-rare. Remove from the oven and let rest 10 minutes.

3   Meanwhile, slice the rolls in half horizontally. Spread 2 tablespoons of fig spread on the bottom half of each roll. Evenly divide the soft Brie between the rolls.

4   Thinly slice the steak and divide it evenly among the 6 sandwiches. Top the steak with 3 to 4 tablespoons of the Balsamic Onions. Put the top halves of the rolls on the sandwiches and gently press down so the buns absorb all of the juices from the meat and the onions. Slice in half and serve hot or at room temperature.

Chocolate Peanut Butter Brownies

These bars are going to blow your mind! Rich and chewy dark chocolate brownies, studded with salty peanuts and little chunks of semi-sweet chocolate chips are topped with a sweet, creamy peanut butter layer and to fish it off, a thick glossy coating of dark chocolate ganache. There is, indeed, some busy work involved in making these, but it is so well worth it to get these show-stopping brownies, which practically look as though they have been cut with a laser. Because they're so rich, I cut small portions, but feel free to make them monster-sized, too!

MAKES 24 BROWNIES
PREP TIME: 1 HOUR
  (including freezer time)
COOK TIME: 1 HOUR

BROWNIES

12 tablespoons
  unsalted butter,
  at room temperature

1¼ cups sugar

1 tablespoon
  vanilla extract

2 large eggs

½ cup all-purpose flour

¾ cup unsweetened
  dark cocoa powder

½ teaspoon kosher salt

2 cups salted roasted
  peanuts

PEANUT BUTTER LAYER

1⅓ cups powdered sugar

¼ cup creamy
  peanut butter

3 tablespoons milk

GANACHE

1½ cups heavy cream

1 pound dark semi-sweet
  chocolate pieces

1 Preheat the oven to 325°F. Line the bottom of a 8 x 8 x 2-inch baking dish with 2 sheets of foil, crisscrossing them so that there is overhang on all 4 sides. Spray the top of the foil and the foil-lined sides of the pan with baking spray.

2 In a small saucepan over medium heat, melt the butter and cook until it reaches a deep golden brown color, 5 to 7 minutes.

3 In the bowl of a standing mixer fitted with the paddle attachment, whip the butter, sugar and vanilla on medium speed until light and fluffy, about 3 minutes. Beat in the eggs, one at a time, until they are well combined.

4 Sift the flour, cocoa and salt together in a bowl, then slowly add them to the batter, mixing until it is just combined. Add the peanuts and fold them in by hand with a spatula or spoon.

5 Transfer the batter to the prepared pan and spread evenly to the edges. Bake for about 28 minutes. Do not overbake!

6 When the brownies are cool enough to touch, put them in the freezer, still in the pan, for 20 minutes.

7 Meanwhile, make the peanut butter layer and the chocolate ganache. To make the peanut butter layer, in a medium bowl, combine and whip together the powdered sugar, peanut butter and milk with an electric mixer until fluffy. Set aside.

8   For the ganache, bring the cream to a simmer in a saucepan over medium heat. Remove from the heat and add the chocolate pieces. Let sit for about 5 minutes, then whisk until smooth and glossy. Set aside to cool.

9   Remove the brownies from the freezer and, using an offset spatula, smooth the peanut butter layer over the brownies. (I used a tiny bit of water on the spatula to get the peanut butter layer extra smooth.) Return the brownies to the freezer for 20 minutes more.

10 Remove the brownies from the freezer and spread the ganache evenly over the top. Return them to the freezer for about 1 hour.

11 Gently loosen the foil from the baking pan with a spatula, and then, using the foil overhangs, lift the brownies out of the baking dish and peel the foil off, leaving a huge block of brownies. Place them on a cutting board. Trim off the edges, and then slice the brownies using a large, sharp knife. (I like to run the knife under hot water after every couple of cuts to keep the slices really clean.) Store the brownie in an airtight container in the refrigerator until ready to serve. (I prefer to bring them to room temperature before serving.)

AUTUMN

Open House Brunch

MENU

- PUMPKIN CINNAMON ROLLS WITH VANILLA CREAM CHEESE FROSTING

- CHICKEN APPLE SAUSAGE

- BAKED EGGS WITH SQUASH, KALE AND CHEDDAR

We are known for the huge open house brunch that we throw at our home on Thanksgiving weekend each year. Because so many friends and family are in town, it is a great time to see everyone.

My Pumpkin Cinnamon Rolls define this annual brunch. I bake them by the dozen and leave them hot on the kitchen counter for any friends that should wander in throughout the morning. I also make the Chicken Apple Sausage the day before and warm the delicious patties as guests arrive.

This past year, I included a baked egg dish. Besides being beautiful and seasonal, it is also incredibly easy to prepare in large quantities ahead of time. Only the cracking of the eggs and the baking are left for the last minute.

I always include carafes of hot coffee and steamed milk, as well as pitchers of cold orange juice and a never-ending supply of Spicy Bloody Marys (page 70).

PREPARING A BRUNCH AHEAD OF TIME

For this menu, I like to make the cinnamon-roll dough the night before, and after it has risen, I stick it in the refrigerator. In the morning, I let it come to room temperature by leaving it somewhere warm. Continue on, letting the dough rest and rise for the second time before the rolls are baked. You have just saved yourself hours the morning of your brunch. You can also make the frosting the day before and refrigerate it. Take it out at the same time as the dough so it can warm up to room temperature as well—it will spread more easily that way.

The sausage patties can also be made the day before, and frankly, marinating in their flavors will only enhance their tastiness. Just fry and bake them the morning of the brunch.

I also recommend having backup pitchers of juice and bloody Marys in the refrigerator. I like to make all the mess at once before the guests have arrived rather than fussing with mixing the bloody Mary recipe while they are there. So, that means having extra supplies somewhere, even if it is in Tupperware. Just discretely transfer to the serving pitcher. If you have a drink dispenser with a spigot, that is always my favorite route. They hold a ton of beverage and guests can serve themselves. For my Bloody Mary recipe, see page 70.

Pumpkin Cinnamon Rolls with Vanilla Cream Cheese Frosting

Cinnamon rolls are one of my very favorite foods, but I took great joy in lending these a seasonal touch with the addition of pumpkin. Not only do they take on a wonderful orange color, but the taste and added moisture from the pumpkin make these especially wonderful. I am in gooey cinnamon roll camp. I like them buttery and sugary and slathered in frosting. If you are going to go for it, go all the way. That means tons of butter and sugar and cinnamon in the filling. I like it to melt and ooze out in the baking process just to ensure a little extra goodness in the bottom of the pan.

The crowning touch on these gorgeous rolls is the Vanilla Cream Cheese Frosting. The tanginess of the cream cheese is perfect with the pumpkin and balances out the intense sweetness of the rolls' filling. If you make these for friends and family once, you will be making them by popular demand forever.

MAKES 12 HUGE ROLLS
PREP TIME: 2 HOURS
COOK TIME: 35 MINUTES

1 cup whole milk

1 cup plus
  2 tablespoons sugar

two ¼-ounce packages
  yeast

½ cup (1 stick) unsalted
  butter

1 teaspoon salt

1 cup pumpkin puree

2 large eggs

8 cups all-purpose flour

FILLING

1 cup plus 2 tablespoons
  unsalted butter

2 cups sugar

3 teaspoons cinnamon

1 In a small saucepan over low heat, heat ½ cup of the milk and the 2 tablespoons of sugar until the sugar has disintegrated. Transfer to a small bowl. When the milk cools to 110°F, sprinkle in the yeast. Set aside for about 20 minutes, for the yeast to rise and puff.

2 In a small saucepan over medium heat, combine the remaining 1 cup sugar and ½ cup milk, butter and salt. Cook, stirring until everything is melted and well combined, about 5 minutes. Remove from the heat and transfer to the bowl of a standing mixer fitted with the dough hook.

3 With the mixer on low speed, add in the pumpkin puree and mix until well incorporated. Add the eggs, one at a time, and mix well. Add the yeast mixture.

4 With the mixer running on low speed, add the flour, 1 cup at a time. After you have added all the flour, increase the speed to medium and keep mixing until you have a smooth dough, 3 to 4 minutes.

5 Grease a large mixing bowl and transfer the dough to the bowl. Cover the top of the bowl with plastic wrap and put the bowl somewhere warm and draft free. Let the dough rise for at least 1 hour, and up to 3 hours.

6 For the filling, melt the butter in a small saucepan over medium heat until it has turned golden brown, about 10 minutes. Set aside.

7 On a lightly floured surface, roll the dough out into a large rectangle, about ¼ inch thick. Brush the browned butter over the dough evenly.

**VANILLA CREAM
    CHEESE FROSTING**

8 ounces cream cheese

2 cups powdered sugar

2 tablespoons whole milk

2 teaspoons vanilla extract

8   Mix the sugar and cinnamon together in a medium bowl and then sprinkle over the browned butter. Gently roll the dough up into a large log. Slice the log into 12 rolls and place them on a parchment-lined baking sheet. Cover with plastic wrap and let rise again, in a warm and draft free place, for at least 30 minutes.

9   Preheat the oven to 350°F.

10 Brush the cinnamon rolls with the melted butter and then bake for 30 minutes.

11 Meanwhile, make the vanilla cream cheese frosting: In a mixing bowl, beat the cream cheese with the powdered sugar, milk and vanilla until fluffy, about 2 minutes. Refrigerate in an airtight container for up to 5 days, until ready to use.

12 As soon as the cinnamon rolls come out of the oven, slather them with frosting, which will melt over the hot rolls. Serve immediately or at room temperature.

Chicken Apple Sausage

This is a fast and easy homemade sausage that makes the most of lean ground chicken. Ripe apples and onions along with some fresh parsley and fennel seed coax the chicken into a surprisingly sweet and savory breakfast sausage that is a wonderful accompaniment to almost any breakfast you can dream up.

MAKE AHEAD: You can prepare these sausages up to 1 day before frying them. Wrap in plastic and refrigerate.

SERVES 4 TO 6
PREP TIME: 10 MINUTES
COOK TIME: 25 MINUTES

2 tablespoons butter

1 yellow onion, small diced

1 apple, peeled and
    small diced

2 pounds ground chicken

1 tablespoon fresh
    thyme leaves

1 tablespoon fennel seeds

kosher salt

vegetable oil, for cooking

1   In a large pan, melt the butter over medium heat. Add the onion and cook until soft and tender, about 5 minutes. Add the apple, stir to combine, and cook for another 5 minutes.

2   Put the ground chicken in a large mixing bowl. Add the onion and apple mixture, thyme and fennel seeds. When cool enough to handle, mix really well with clean hands. Form a small patty and fry it in a little vegetable oil in a pan so that you can taste for salt. Season with salt if necessary. Form all of the chicken mixture into 3-inch round patties (you will have about 12).

3   Preheat the oven to 350°F.

4   Heat a pan over medium heat and add a few teaspoons of vegetable oil. Cook the patties in batches, browning them on both sides, about 2 minutes per side. As you finish browning each chicken patty, place them on a sheet pan. When the patties have all been browned, bake them for 10 minutes. Serve immediately.

Baked Eggs with Squash, Kale and Cheddar

I love the ease of baked eggs as well as the flexibility to flavor them with whatever seasonal ingredients are the most delicious at the particular moment. In autumn, my favorite additions are earthy squash, sweet red onion and hearty kale. I like to cook the eggs so that the yolks are still runny and can be stirred into the vegetables for added creaminess. A dusting of white Cheddar makes these baked eggs extra comforting. With all the bright orange squash and dark green leafy kale, this dish is also very nutritious. All of those healthy vitamins make me feel like I can justify eating two pumpkin cinnamon rolls slathered in frosting for dessert. Because the wholesomeness of the egg dish would completely balance that out, right?

SERVES 4 TO 6
PREP TIME: 10 MINUTES
COOK TIME: 25 MINUTES

8 large eggs

3 tablespoons unsalted butter

1 red onion, thinly sliced

kosher salt

2 cups squash, peeled and diced (acorn, delicata, butternut)

1 head curly kale, stems discarded, leaves torn into bite-sized pieces (about 2 cups)

1 cup shredded white Cheddar cheese

2 teaspoons fresh thyme leaves, plus 4 to 6 sprigs for garnish

1   Preheat the oven to 400°F.

2   Gently crack the eggs into a bowl, taking care not to break the yolks. Set aside.

3   In an ovenproof skillet, melt the butter over low heat. Add the onion and sprinkle with salt. Sweat the onion over medium heat until it begins to soften, 3 to 4 minutes. Add the squash and stir to coat with the butter and onions. Cook until the squash is tender, but not falling apart, about 6 minutes.

4   Add the kale and cook for 2 minutes, or until it turns bright green and tender. Sprinkle the vegetables with the Cheddar, and then very gently pour the eggs over the vegetables and cheese, spreading the eggs out so that they each cook separately. Sprinkle the fresh thyme over the eggs.

5   Bake in the oven for 10 to 12 minutes, until the egg whites are set but the yolks are still runny.

6   To serve, scoop an egg along with some squash, kale and onions onto each plate. Garnish with a sprig of thyme and serve immediately.

CHAPTER FOUR

Winter

Winter is all about family, holiday festivities, crackling fires, and lots and lots of baking! With a never-ending stream of cookies and candy in and out of my oven, our house is constantly full of treats. My preparation for Christmas is a month-long indulgence of decorating and loud Christmas music. My husband just shakes his head as December 1st marks the immediate delivery of several Christmas trees, making gingerbread houses with the girls, and generally pure giddiness for me. Thousands of lights unfurl, and the girls and I squeal with delight unpacking the decorations and trimming the tree. As far as food goes, we call December "gluttony month." After New Year's, we reel it in a bit, hibernating and hanging out with close friends for laid-back times like our Family Dinner.

WINTER MENUS

Family Dinner

MENU

- CHIVE BREAD

- PETE'S RIGATONI BOLOGNESE

- EJ'S CAESAR SALAD

- APPLE CINNAMON OATMEAL CRISP

Sometimes you are lucky enough to marry into your best friends. And when my husband Pete and I got married, that is exactly what happened to me. I knew I had stumbled into a special group of people as soon as I met his high school buddies and their beautiful wives, but what I didn't know was that some friends can truly grow into extensions of your family. Every eight weeks or so, we all gather at one of our houses and have what we simply call Family Dinner. The children run free in the house and all of the adults gather in the kitchen to drink wine, laugh and cook dinner together. Everything is casual, and the whole house is filled with laughter. The women can retire to the den to chat and tell our little ones to "ask Daddy" when they need something. This is one of my very favorite family dinner menus, which we have eaten winter after winter, and one of the few times where the men are in charge—all I have to make is the bread and dessert!

Chive Bread

This bread is my spin on traditional garlic bread. Chives are a bit of an anomaly in the Pacific Northwest: with the exception of rosemary, they are the only herb that I have access to in my own garden just about all year round. They never disappoint me! However, if you live in a region with harsher winters, they are also widely available in grocery stores all year round. I love chives—their wonderful mild onion flavor is distinctive without being overwhelming. Mixed with melted butter and spooned over rustic ciabatta bread, this is a wonderful upgrade from your usual garlic bread. Pair it with pasta or dunk it in sauces, soups and chowders.

SERVES 4 TO 6
PREP TIME: 5 MINUTES
COOK TIME: 12 MINUTES

½ cup (1 stick) unsalted butter

1 loaf rustic ciabatta bread, split in half horizontally

½ cup finely minced chives

pinch of kosher salt

1　Preheat the oven to 400°F.

2　In a small saucepan, melt the butter. Gently mix in the chives and salt with a spoon.

3　Place 2 pieces of ciabatta on a baking sheet, cut sides up. Spoon half of the melted butter mixture on each half. Reassemble the ciabatta, placing the top on the bottom, and bake for 10 minutes, until the bread is hot and crispy and the inside is soft and buttery.

4　Slice and serve immediately.

Pete's Rigatoni Bolognese

This sauce is something to behold and I have to give my husband Pete the credit. He may not cook often, but when he does, it is quite a production and quite the result! This Bolognese is something that he spent an entire winter perfecting to have just the right flavors, and now it is something that all of our friends and family look forward to. And, while Pete is not so secretly waiting for Bobby Flay to burst through our kitchen door and demand a Bolognese "throwdown," for now it is only our friends kicking the door down to get at this unbelievable sauce. Yours will be too.

SERVES 6 TO 8
PREP TIME: 20 MINUTES / COOK TIME: 2 HOURS

PETE'S BOLOGNESE SAUCE

4 ounces pancetta, chopped

8 ounces Italian sausage, spicy

8 ounces ground pork

8 ounces ground veal

1½ cups minced yellow onion

⅔ cup minced carrots

⅔ cup minced celery

⅔ cup minced zucchini

⅔ cup minced mushrooms

4 garlic cloves, minced

2 tablespoons fresh
    basil leaves, torn

2 teaspoons fresh thyme leaves

1 tablespoon dried oregano

1 bay leaf

1 teaspoon red pepper flakes

½ teaspoon ground nutmeg

¼ teaspoon ground allspice

3 ounces tomato paste

¼ cup water

¾ cup red wine

two 28-ounce cans crushed
    tomatoes

4 tablespoons salted butter

1 large Parmesan rind

¼ cup heavy cream

2 tablespoons sugar

kosher salt

1 pound rigatoni pasta

2 to 3 cups freshly grated
    Parmesan, for serving

1. In a large heavy pot, crisp the pancetta over medium heat, rendering the fat, 7 to 8 minutes.

2. Add the sausage (squeezed out of the casing) and lightly brown. Add the ground pork and veal and cook until lightly browned, stirring frequently, about 10 minutes. Drain off the extra fat, leaving the meat in the pot. Add the chopped vegetables, herbs and spices and sweat, about 10 minutes.

3. Stir in the tomato paste and water, then stir in the wine. Stir in the crushed tomatoes and let the sauce simmer and the flavors blend for 5 to 10 minutes.

4. Add the butter and Parmesan rind, cover, and decrease the heat to low. Simmer the sauce, stirring occasionally, for at least 1 hour, preferably more.

5. Use an immersion blender to puree the sauce to a smooth consistency. Fish out the bay leaf and the Parmesan rind and stir in the cream. Taste and adjust the seasoning with sugar and salt.

6. Cook the rigatoni to al dente in a large pot of salted boiling water, according to package directions.

7. Toss the Bolognese sauce with the rigatoni and serve with freshly grated Parmesan cheese and a bowl of extra Bolognese sauce.

INGREDIENT NOTE: Please use a wine that you would be happy to drink for this sauce, as its flavor will only intensify as the sauce cooks.

EJ's Caesar Salad

Every time our dear friend EJ gets into the kitchen, we beg him to make his Caesar salad. It is light and zesty with great garlic flavor and a nutty anchovy undertone. We toss his dressing with hearts of romaine lettuce and my buttery Garlicky Croutons and there is never a leaf left in the bottom of the bowl. His dressing is always best after he has an extra glass of wine, so I plied him with wine before I hopped into the kitchen to record exactly what he was up to in there!

INGREDIENT NOTE: EJ attributes his salad's success to the following ingredients, which will help yours to be the best, too! He insists on EXTRA LIGHT olive oil, so that the olive taste doesn't overwhelm the dressing. Even if the thought of anchovy paste makes you nervous, use it here as it's an integral part of the dressing!

MAKE AHEAD: The croutons can be made in the morning—just cover with a dishcloth and leave at room temperature.

SERVES 4 TO 6
PREP TIME: 5 MINUTES
COOK TIME: 12 MINURTES

CAESAR DRESSING

1 large egg

1 garlic clove, minced

½ teaspoon Worcestershire sauce

1 teaspoon red wine vinegar

½ teaspoon Dijon mustard

2 tablespoons lemon juice

1 heaping tablespoon anchovy paste

⅓ cup Parmesan cheese, finely grated

¾ cup extra light olive oil

kosher salt and freshly ground black pepper

GARLICKY CROUTONS

2 cups cubed ciabatta or Italian bread

2 tablespoons unsalted butter

2 tablespoons olive oil

3 cloves garlic, minced

kosher salt

3 romaine hearts, chopped into bite-size pieces

1 cup Parmesan cheese, finely grated

1   First make the Caeser dressing: Bring a small pan of water to a simmer. Add the egg and cook for 30 seconds. (Coddling the egg not only gives the dressing a creamy texture, it also soothes any fears about using raw egg.)

2   Crack the egg into a medium bowl. Add the garlic, Worcestershire sauce, vinegar, mustard, lemon juice and anchovy paste. Whisk well until smooth. Whisk in the Parmesan. Continuing to whisk, add the olive oil in a thin stream until the dressing has thickened and emulsified. Season with salt and pepper. Refrigerate until ready to use. Extra dressing can be refrigerated for up to 2 days.

3   Next make the garlicky croutons: Over medium-low heat, melt the butter and oil together in a saucepan. Add the garlic and a sprinkle of salt and cook for about 1 minute, until the garlic is slightly tender. Add the bread cubes and toss with the oil and butter until evenly coated. Toast gently, until the croutons are golden brown, about 5 minutes. Take care not to burn the garlic! Transfer the croutons with all the garlic bits to a plate and set aside.

4   To assemble the salad, in a large bowl, combine the romaine hearts and just enough dressing to coat the lettuce after tossing. Add the croutons and toss again. Top the salad with the freshly grated Parmesan cheese and provide tongs so guests can serve themselves.

Apple Cinnamon Oatmeal Crisp

This is one of my most beloved and most often made family recipes. It traces back to my grandma Grace, and I have been making this since I was a child (literally.) My daughters know what I am making as soon as I take the big tub of oats out. Pia and Coco help me with this dessert all the time, working on their measuring and stirring skills. This is go-to fruit crisp can be made any time of year with seasonal fruit. The topping is a crumbly brown sugar and oats combination—made extra tender with the addition of shortening—that complements anything from berries to apples. This is wonderful served at room temperature, or hot with a scoop of vanilla ice cream.

GENEROUS TIP: I recommend placing your baking dish on a sheet pan in case the fruit bubbles over.

SERVES 8 TO 10
PREP TIME: 15 MINUTES
COOK TIME: 45 MINUTES

1½ tablespoons plus
   2 teaspoons butter

1 cup all-purpose flour

½ teaspoon baking soda

½ teaspoon salt

1½ teaspoons cinnamon

½ cup brown sugar

1 cup oats

½ cup vegetable shortening

2½ to 3 pounds apples,
   peeled, cored and sliced
   into thin wedges
   (about 6 cups)

1   Preheat the oven to 350°F. Grease a 9 x 13 x 2-inch baking dish with the 2 teaspoons of butter and place it on a sheet pan.

2   In a medium bowl, mix all of the dry ingredients together until well combined. Add the shortening and work it in with a pastry cutter or, using your clean hands, mix the dough together until it resembles a coarse crumb.

3   Sprinkle about a third of the crumbly dough on the bottom of the baking dish. Mound the apples in the pan and sprinkle the rest of the dough over the fruit. Dot the top of the crisp with the remaining 1½ tablespoons butter.

4   Place the sheet pan in the oven and bake the apple crisp for about 45 minutes, or until the fruit is bubbling and the topping is golden.

5   Serve immediately or at room temperature.

Snow Day Lunch

MENU

- CHEDDAR AND GREEN ONION BUTTERMILK BISCUITS

- SPLIT PEA SOUP

- PUMPKIN CHICKEN CHILI

- PEANUT BUTTER CARAMEL CORN

- MOLASSES COOKIES

Snow happens in Seattle, it just happens rarely. And, when the swirling purple skies do bring snow, it literally shuts the city down. No one goes to work and we are all trapped in our respective neighborhoods. I am unbelievably lucky that not only friends, but two of my sibling live within a few blocks of me. So, even when the cars can't brave the slippery hills, we still man-age to pack our house with friends and family!

Nothing gives me greater joy than getting every fireplace in the house crackling, filling my kitchen with people I love, and looking out the window to see my little bundled-up babies building snowmen. I leave big pots of soup and chili, bubbling away on the stovetop and put out a basket of hot biscuits—perfect for sopping up the bottom of the soup bowl.

And, you can't have a snow day without movies and sweet baked goods. I suggest a platter of chewy Molasses Cookies, and a big bowl of my Peanut Butter Caramel Corn for maximum delight.

ENTERTAINING WITH A SIMMERING SOUP BAR

Making big batches of soup and homemade biscuits (see page 166) or rolls (see page 175) is a great format for casual entertaining. I often make a few different types of chili for at-home tail-gating parties. You just leave them hot on the stovetop and set out a condiment bar full of chili toppings. I also serve soups like this for tree trimming with family during the holidays. It is an easy way to entertain because the whole meal can be pre-made up to the day before, and the host has to do pretty much nothing for the guests except set out condiments, bowls and spoons.

GIFTING CARAMEL CORN

Caramel corn, and the many, many different spins you can put on it, makes an ideal homemade gift. I add cranberries and dark chocolate for the holidays, pastel candies and white chocolate for Easter, and so on. You can present it simply in cellophane bags or clear acrylic boxes or package it up in pretty tins for a delicious and heartfelt gift that is easy to make in large quantities.

Cheddar and Green Onion Buttermilk Biscuits

A fluffy biscuit is a wonderful thing. But take that biscuit and add sharp Cheddar cheese and fresh green onion and you have an entirely different level of comfort. These tender flavorful biscuits are great on their own or slathered with butter, partnered with eggs at breakfast, or dunked in a hearty soup.

MAKES 14 BISCUITS
PREP TIME: 10 MINUTES
COOK TIME: 10 MINUTES

2 cups all-purpose flour,
   plus more for rolling

1 tablespoon sugar

4 teaspoons baking powder

1 teaspoon salt

¼ cup (½ stick) cold salted
   butter, cut into small pieces

¼ cup vegetable shortening

⅔ cup buttermilk

1 large egg

2 cups shredded Cheddar
   cheese

½ cup sliced green onions

1 Preheat the oven to 400°F. Line a sheet pan with a silpat liner or parchment paper.

2 In the bowl of a food processor, pulse together the dry ingredients.

3 Add the butter and the shortening and pulse until you have a crumbly dough.

4 In a separate bowl, whisk together the buttermilk and egg. With the food processor on, stream in the buttermilk and egg mixture until the dough has just come together. Pulse in the cheese and green onions for 2 seconds.

5 Turn out the dough onto a lightly floured surface. Use the flour to knead the dough into a ball, making sure the cheese and green onion are well incorporated into the dough.

6 Using a rolling pin, roll the dough out to about ½ inch thick. Use a 3-inch biscuit cutter or jelly glass to cut out 14 biscuits. Transfer the biscuits to the prepared sheet pan and bake for 10 minutes, or until golden on top.

7 Transfer the biscuits to a cooling rack. Serve immediately or at room temperature.

Split Pea Soup

When I was growing up, if I saw a big chocolate cake on the counter when I got home from school, I knew my mom had made split pea soup. My brothers and sister couldn't stand it—hence the dessert bribery—but I just loved it! So, I always had a big bowl of this delicious soup, and then grinned as I was the first to enjoy an extra-big slice of chocolate cake. Split pea soup is filling and hearty and the smoky, salty ham hock adds fantastic background flavor. As my mother would say, "It will stick to your ribs!" And, unlike my siblings, my own young children devour this soup without a second thought.

GENEROUS TIP: Do NOT add any salt or pepper to this recipe until the very end—
the ham is very salty, and chances are you won't need any additioal salt at all.

SERVES 4 TO 6
PREP TIME: 15 MINUTES
COOK TIME: 1 HOUR 10 MINUTES

¼ cup olive oil

1 yellow onion, finely chopped

3 carrots, finely chopped

3 celery ribs, finely chopped

1 pound smoked ham hock

1 pound green split peas, rinsed and drained

2 quarts chicken stock

kosher salt and freshly ground black pepper

1 In a soup pot, heat the olive oil over medium heat. Add the onion, carrots and celery. Stir to coat the vegetables and cook for 5 minutes, until soft.

2 Add the whole ham hock, split peas and chicken stock. Decrease the heat to low and simmer for about an hour, or until the peas are soft and the ham hock is tender.

3 Transfer the ham hock to a cutting board. With a small knife, trim all of the lean, usable meat off the bone, then cut the meat into very small pieces and set aside. Discard the bone and fat.

4 Using an immersion blender, puree about two-thirds of the soup until somewhat smooth. Add the ham pieces to the soup and cook over low heat until the soup has thickened slightly, 5 to 8 minutes. Now taste and adjust the seasoning with salt and pepper, if desired.

5 Serve immediately.

Pumpkin Chicken Chili

My chicken chili has a bit of a cult following among my friends, but I am always looking for ways to improve and improvise on the recipe. This Pumpkin Chicken Chili is a perfect example. With pumpkin and sweet potatoes, I created a new and different chili full of unexpected ingredients. Layers of wonderful flavors, and a fantastic shade of orange, may make this chili the new cult favorite.

SERVES 4 TO 6
PREP TIME: 15 MINUTES
COOK TIME: 40 MINUTES

2 bone-in chicken breasts, skin on

kosher salt

2 tablespoons salted butter

1 yellow onion, chopped

1 small sugar pumpkin, peeled, seeded and chopped

2 large sweet potatoes, peeled and chopped

three 15-ounce cans white beans, rinsed and drained

2 quarts chicken stock

2 teaspoons ground cumin

1 teaspoon chili powder

½ teaspoon red pepper flakes

1 tablespoon red wine vinegar

sour cream and thinly sliced green onions, for garnish

1   Preheat the oven to 375°F.

2   On a sheet pan, arrange the chicken breasts and sprinkle with salt on both sides. Roast the chicken for 30 minutes.

3   Meanwhile, melt the butter in a large soup pot over medium heat. Add the onion and sweat over medium heat until softened, 5 minutes. Add the pumpkin and sweet potato and stir well. Cook for 5 to 6 minutes, until tender, but not mushy. Add the white beans, followed by the chicken stock. Cover and simmer over low heat while you wait for the chicken to finish roasting.

4   When the chicken is finished, pull the skin off of the breast, using tongs or a fork so you don't burn yourself. Shred the chicken off of the bone and into bite-size pieces. Discard the skin, bones and fat and add the chicken to the soup pot.

5   Stir in the cumin, chili powder, red pepper flakes and vinegar and simmer, uncovered, for 10 minutes, or until slightly thickened. Season with salt.

6   Serve immediately, or reheat over low heat until bubbling, 5 to 7 minutes and serve hot. Garnish with the sour cream and green onions.

Peanut Butter Caramel Corn

I've said it once, and I am sure I will say it again: Caramel corn is my kryptonite. If I make a batch, there is no staying away from it. However, with or without the self-control of a normal person, this is one of the best sweet snacks I could ever imagine. You can add all types of mix-ins, too. When the caramel corn is fresh from the oven, I will toss in anything from honey-roasted peanuts to M&Ms to make this even more indulgent. But truth be told—my favorite way to eat it is plain.

GENEROUS TIP: Because this recipe keeps for 10 days in an airtight container, it makes a great gift to send by post. Getting it out the door also prevents me from eating it all and turning green from too much sugar!

MAKES 16 CUPS
PREP TIME: 5 MINUTES
COOK TIME: 1 HOUR 15 MINUTES

POCORN

¼ cup vegetable oil

1 cup organic popping corn

kosher salt

PEANUT BUTTER CARAMEL

1 cup (2 sticks) unsalted butter

2 cups light brown sugar

½ cup light corn syrup

½ cup creamy peanut butter

1 teaspoon kosher salt

½ teaspoon baking soda

1 teaspoon vanilla extract

INGREDIENT NOTE: If there is a nut allergy in the family, simply omit the peanut butter for a still-perfect caramel corn!

1 Preheat the oven to 250°F.

2 First make the popcorn: Put a large pot over medium heat, and add the oil and popcorn. Place a lid on the pot, slightly askew, so that steam can escape. Pop the corn until there are a few seconds between pops, and it sounds like they are mostly cooked.

3 Pour the popped corn into a large roasting pan (like one you would use to roast a turkey) and sprinkle with kosher salt.

4 In the same pot that you made the popcorn, melt the butter, brown sugar, corn syrup, peanut butter and salt. Bring to a boil, stirring, for 7 minutes.

5 In a tiny bowl, mix the baking soda and vanilla together until the baking soda is mostly dissolved.

6 Remove the pot from the heat, and stir in the vanilla and baking soda mixture. The caramel should be very light and frothy. Immediately pour the caramel over the popcorn, and gently fold the caramel into the popcorn to coat it. (At this point you might think there is not enough caramel for the corn, as there will be globs of caramel, and a lot of the popcorn will not seem well coated. But don't worry! There will be plenty.)

7 Bake the caramel corn for 15 minutes. Remove the roasting pan from the oven and gently stir the popcorn into the melting caramel until the popcorn is better coated. Return to the oven for another 15 minutes, after which the popcorn should be evenly coated with the caramel.

8 Return the caramel corn to the oven and bake for a final 15 minutes. Remove from the oven and give the corn one final stir to coat thoroughly. Let cool completely, about 30 minutes.

9 When the popcorn is totally cool, it will have a nice, thin, crispy coating. Serve immediately or store in airtight containers for up to 10 days.

Molasses Cookies

When I think of holiday baking, this is the very first cookie that comes to mind. This recipe comes from Grandma Grace, my mother's mother, and the women in my family have been making these for as long as I can remember. The dough is filled with the flavor of spices and dark molasses, and the cookies bake up wonderfully crispy and sugary on the outside and tender and soft on the inside.

MAKE AHEAD: These cookies can be made ahead. Just store in an airtight container for up to 1 week or freeze for up to 2 months. Thaw to room temperature before serving.

MAKES 2 DOZEN COOKIES
PREP TIME: 5 MINUTES
COOK TIME: 10 MINUTES

¾ cup vegetable shortening

1 cup sugar, plus more for rolling

2 tablespoons dark molasses

1 large egg

2 cups all-purpose flour

1½ teaspoons baking soda

½ teaspoon kosher salt

1 teaspoon ground cinnamon

½ teaspoon ground ginger

½ teaspoon ground allspice

1   Preheat the oven to 375°F. Prepare 2 baking sheets with parchment paper.

2   In the bowl of a standing mixer, beat together the shortening, sugar, molasses, and egg until light and fluffy, 2 to 3 minutes.

3   In a separate bowl, combine the flour, baking soda, salt and spices. Add the dry ingredients to the shortening mixture, and beat until well combined.

4   Using your hands, roll tablespoons of the dough into balls. Roll the balls in a bowl of sugar until covered and set each ball on the baking sheet about 3 inches apart. Press the balls flat with the palm of your hand.

5   Bake the cookies for 8 to 10 minutes and then transfer to a cooling rack. Serve immediately.

Holiday Dinner Party

MENU

- BRIE EN CROUTE WITH DRIED APRICOT CHUTNEY

- ROSEMARY DINNER ROLLS

- HOLIDAY SALAD

- STRING BEANS WITH CRISPY SHALLOTS

- CELERY ROOT WHIPPED POTATOES

- ROASTED BEEF TENDERLOIN WITH PARSLEY CREAM SAUCE

- CHOCOLATE RASPBERRY TART

I can only reason that my obsession with Christmas stems from my joyful childhood memories. I feel compelled to make sure my own children have the same giddy feelings about Christmas and the whole season of giving and sharing. Also I just like an excuse to decorate every possible surface in my house with glitter and fake snow.

For me, the holidays are about the decorations, the baking, the music, and most of all, the gathering of family around the table. While everyday celebrations are important and joyful, I always treat Christmas Eve dinner like the Super Bowl of family gatherings. It matters to me, a lot. It is the only occasion of the year when I am guaranteed to see everyone in my family, and many family friends to boot. It is a chance for me to give back to them in the best way that I know how—with food.

HOLIDAY TABLE DÉCOR

If there is ever an occasion to set a beautiful and special table, it is for the holiday season—the time of year that most of us are called on to really entertain, as well as the time spent together that friends and family remember most. I'm all for putting in a little extra effort! Since I am a huge fan of incorporating unconventional items into table décor, I included costume jewelry here. I have salvaged tons from tag sales over the years, and take delight in scoring these inexpensive and easy-to-find little gems. I tie them around napkins with ribbons, hot glue them to vases and even tuck them into flower arrangements for a little added sparkle. They are unique and special and will give tremendous personality to your holiday table—plus they can be reused again and again.

TIP FROM MY MOTHER: "HEAT YOUR PLATES!"

Let's just say my mom engrained quite a few things in our brains as children, um, as far as entertaining was concerned (and otherwise!). One that stands out is this rule— "heat your plates!" There is nothing like piling your beautiful hot food onto a cold serving platter or dinner plate to seriously put a damper on how delicious it was supposed to be. I choose the oven as my tool. I either turn it on very low, and then turn it off before placing the plates in for a few minutes. Or, as soon as you are done cooking, you can stick the plates in the oven for 1 minute, and then carefully remove them making sure they aren't going to burn anyone before you serve!

If you are serving hot soup, you can use this same technique for the bowls. Or fill the bowls with a bit of hot water from a teakettle and let the water sit and heat up the bowls. Then dump the water and dry the bowls right before dishing up the hot soup.

Brie en Croute with Dried Apricot Chutney

This is a revival appetizer—it was very popular in the 1980s and I am bringing it back with a spin. Don't get me wrong, between buttery puff pastry and creamy Brie cheese, there isn't much to complain about! But when you surprise people with a layer of tart and savory Dried Apricot Chutney, it is delicious on a whole new level. When you cut into the crispy pastry, the chutney oozes out on a river of melted Brie. Quick! Get the crackers!

MAKE AHEAD: The dried apricot chutney can be made 1 to 2 days ahead of time and kept in the refrigerator.

SERVES 4 TO 6
PREP TIME: 5 MINUTES
COOK TIME: 15 MINUTES

DRIED APRICOT CHUTNEY

1 tablespoon unsalted butter

½ cup minced onions

kosher salt

½ cup finely chopped dried apricots

½ cup white wine

1 sheet puff pastry

1 wheel Brie, chilled

1 large egg

2 teaspoons water

1 package of your favorite crackers or 1 baguette, for serving

1 First make the dried apricot chutney: In a sauté pan, melt the butter over medium heat. Add the onions and a sprinkle of salt. Cook for 3 minutes, until slightly softened. Add the dried apricots and stir to combine. Add the wine and stir, scraping up all of the browned bits. Reduce the heat to low and cook for 10 minutes, stirring often. Season with salt and transfer to a bowl. Refrigerate the chutney until ready to use.

2 Preheat the oven to 425°F. Line a sheet pan with parchment paper.

3 Spread out the puff pastry and place the wheel of Brie in the center of the sheet. Pile the cold chutney on top of the Brie. Pull the edges of the puff pastry sheet up around the wheel of Brie and bring it together at the top, pinching it closed. Transfer the Brie package to the prepared sheet pan.

4 In a small bowl, beat the egg and water together to create an egg wash. Gently and lightly brush the egg wash over the puff pastry.

5 Bake the Brie until the puff pastry is golden brown and cooked through (the inside will be oozing, melted Brie), about 15 minutes.

6 Transfer to a platter with the crackers or baguette slices and serve immediately.

Rosemary Dinner Rolls

One of the simple joys in life is the smell of freshly baked bread. Once you get the hang of managing the yeast, baking homemade bread and rolls takes on a whole new ease that will make it not only manageable, but enjoyable! I always treat my family and friends to homemade rolls for the holidays. These are best when the dough is made the day of and baked just before eating.

GENEROUS TIP: To heat up your yeast-blooming bowl, run very hot water into the bowl. (If you put hot water in a cold bowl, it will make warm water = no blooming.) Then, with the tap water as hot as it gets, measure a cup of it. Put a thermometer in it if you are in doubt. I like mine around the higher end of the range: 110 to 115°F. Then measure out the hot water into the pre-heated bowl. Proceed with the recipe from there!

MAKES 12 ROLLS
PREP TIME: 20 MINUTES
  (plus 2 hours rising time)
COOK TIME: 20 MINUTES

¼ cup hot water
  (105 to 115°F)

2 teaspoons sugar

one ¼-ounce package
  active dry yeast

6 tablespoons
  unsalted butter,
  plus 3 tablespoons, melted

2 tablespoons freshly minced
  hearty rosemary

1 cup whole milk

3 cups bread flour,
  plus more for rolling

1½ teaspoons kosher salt

1 Stir together the hot water, sugar and the yeast in a small bowl until the yeast is dissolved. Let stand until foamy, at least 10 minutes. (If the mixture does not foam up, throw it out and start over. Your dough will never be right if this step doesn't work.)

2 Melt 6 tablespoons of the butter in a small saucepan over the lowest heat. You don't want the butter to take on any color at all, so keep a watchful eye on the saucepan. Add the rosemary to the butter and let simmer for 1 minute. (The herbs will infuse the butter.) Add the milk and heat just until lukewarm.

3 In the bowl of a standing mixer, mix the yeast mixture with 2 cups of the bread flour and the salt until just combined. Then mix in the milk and butter mixture. With the machine still running, add the last cup of bread flour, a little at a time, and mix the dough until smooth and elastic, 2 to 3 minutes.

4 Transfer the dough to a large, oiled bowl. Cover with plastic wrap and let rest in a warm, draft-free place until doubled in size, at least 1 hour.

5 Transfer the puffy dough ball to a lightly floured surface. Cut the dough in quarters, and then cut each quarter into 3 pieces. Form each of the 12 pieces into little balls and place them, in a single layer, in a dish that has been buttered with 1 tablespoon of the melted butter. Cover them with plastic wrap and let rise for 1 hour.

6 Preheat the oven to 350°F.

7 When the rolls have doubled in size, brush the rolls with the remaining 2 tablespoons melted butter. Bake for about 20 minutes, or until barely golden brown on top.

8 Transfer to a serving dish and serve immediately.

Holiday Salad

This salad aptly earned its name because we serve it every year on Christmas. If salads can be festive, than this one surely is. With tons of delicious toppings and bright colors and flavors, this salad is certain to win a spot at your holiday table as well.

GENEROUS TIP: Whenever you want to use orange pieces in a dish, it is best to "section" them, thus getting rid of any of the peel or pith that might give the sweet juicy orange sections a bitter aftertaste. This technique leaves them looking like little jewels! Using a sharp knife, slice a small amount off the top and bottom of the orange. Next remove the skin and layer of pith underneath, carefully slicing downwards and following the curve of the orange. Continue around the orange, so that in the end, you are left with a shiny ball of the raw fruit with no skin. Carefully cut each section of orange free from the membrane that connects it to the next slice until you have cut free every slice of orange. If making a sauce or dressing to complement the oranges, I always squeeze the remaining juice and pulp from the leftover membranes into a bowl to use later.

MAKE AHEAD: The creamy vinaigrette can be made ahead and refrigerated for up to 3 days.

SERVES 6 TO 8
PREP TIME: 10 MINUTES
COOK TIME: 20 MINUTES

¼ pound thick-cut bacon

2 tablespoons olive oil

2 cups bite-size pieces of rustic sourdough bread

8 cups mixed greens

¼ cup thinly sliced green onions, white and green parts

½ cup thinly sliced fresh mint leaves

½ cup dried cranberries

2 large oranges, sectioned

CREAMY VINAIGRETTE

1 large egg

1 clove garlic

¼ cup red wine vinegar

½ cup olive oil

kosher salt and freshly ground black pepper

1 In a large pan, cook the bacon over medium heat until the fat has been rendered and the bacon is very crispy. Transfer the bacon to a paper towel and set aside. Reserve the bacon fat in the pan.

2 To the pan with the bacon drippings, add the olive oil and stir to combine over medium heat. Add the bread pieces and cook, stirring often, until golden and crispy, about 10 minutes. Set the toasted bread aside.

3 Meanwhile, make the creamy vinaigrette: Bring a small pan of water to a boil. Cook the egg for 3 minutes, until coddled. Remove the egg from the pan and rinse it in cold water. Peel and add the coddled egg to a blender, along with the garlic, vinegar and olive oil. Blend until smooth, then season with salt and pepper. Refrigerate until ready to use.

4 In a large bowl, combine the mixed greens, green onions, mint, dried cranberries, and orange sections. Crumble the reserved bacon over the top of the salad and sprinkle with the toasted bread, adding any little browned bits from the pan the bread was toasted. Toss the salad with the creamy vinaigrette and serve immediately.

String Beans with Crispy Shallots

This is an easy and delicious dish that seems to be equally pleasing to adults and children. Since I am always looking for ways to get my children (and husband) to eat more vegetables, I took notice when this dish went over particularly well with them and my nieces, too. I can't decide if it is the simple, clean flavors of the string beans tossed with just a bit of butter and lemon, or the addition of the crispy fried shallot rings, but something here has just gone terribly right.

SERVES 4 TO 6
PREP TIME: 2 MINUTES
COOK TIME: 12 MINUTES

1 tablespoon unsalted butter

2 tablespoons vegetable oil

1 large shallot, thinly sliced
    into rings

1 pound green beans

1 tablespoon fresh
    lemon juice

kosher salt

1   In a large pan over medium heat, melt the butter and the oil together.

2   Add the shallot rings and cook them over medium heat until they are fried crispy and golden (but not dark) brown, about 5 minutes. Sprinkle with salt and transfer to a paper towel.

3   Add the green beans to the butter and oil and cook, stirring, for 5 to 6 minutes, or until the beans are tender. Add the lemon juice and toss to combine. Season with salt.

4   Transfer the beans to a serving platter and sprinkle with the crispy shallots. Serve immediately.

Celery Root Whipped Potatoes

This is how my mom has been making mashed potatoes my entire life. Incorporating celery root is a trick that she learned from her mother. I can't tell you if it goes back further than that, but let's just say that there is a reason it has survived the test of time. Celery root most definitely adds another layer of flavor that is best described while shoveling more potatoes into your mouth. My meager addition to this family recipe is the cream cheese. It happened by accident, as most delicious things do, when I had run out of butter and needed a substitute. I knew that lots of people add it to their potatoes and I quickly realized why. The extra tanginess and creaminess is as undeniable as my freckles. Delicious.

MAKE AHEAD: These can be made in their entirety the day before and heated up on the stove with the reserved ½ cup cooking liquid or a little water to keep them loose. If your stove is too full with other pots and pans, take a tip from my sister who likes to pile the potatoes into a 9 x 13-inch baking dish, cover them with foil and bake them at 350°F for 20 minutes until piping hot.

SERVES 4 TO 6
PREP TIME: 10 MINUTES
COOK TIME: 25 MINUTES

2 teaspoons kosher salt, plus more for seasoning

3 pounds potatoes, peeled and roughly chopped

¾ pound celery root, peeled, trimmed and roughly chopped

4 ounces cream cheese, cut into pieces

¼ cup (½ stick) unsalted butter, cut into pieces

½ cup buttermilk

freshly ground black pepper

INGREDIENT NOTE: If they are available, I prefer to use Yukon Gold potatoes for their golden color and creamy texture, but any potatoes will do nicely.

1 Fill a large pot halfway with cold water and add the salt, potatoes and celery root. Cover and simmer over medium heat for about 25 minutes, or until the potatoes and celery root are fork-tender.

2 Reserve 1 cup of the cooking liquid, then drain the potatoes and celery root in a strainer.

3 For extra smooth whipped potatoes, run the potatoes and celery root through a food mill before returning them to the pot. Add the cream cheese and the butter and begin to whip with an electric mixer. Add the buttermilk and the reserved cooking liquid and whip until very smooth and fluffy. Season with salt and pepper.

Roasted Beef Tenderloin with Parsley Cream Sauce

Beef tenderloin is most definitely a special occasion dish in our house. It has become a new food tradition in recent years, gracing our Christmas table with its luxurious silky texture and flavor. I add a parsley cream sauce that I can only describe as beautiful. No, wait, I can say more: While initially you will just be amazed by the gorgeous green color, you will soon be charmed by the lovely way that this sauce complements the beef. It doesn't hurt that it is so fast to make that you can pull it together while the meat is resting, resulting in a case of perfect timing!

GENEROUS TIP: The tenderloin needs to sit out for about 30 minutes to come to room temperature before roasting.

SERVES 4 TO 6
PREP TIME: 15 MINUTES
COOK TIME: 35 MINUTES

one 3-pound beef tenderloin, fully trimmed and trussed by your butcher, at room temperature

kosher salt and freshly ground black pepper

PARSLEY CREAM SAUCE

¼ cup (½ stick) unsalted butter

2 shallots, chopped

1 clove garlic

kosher salt

1 cup parsley leaves

½ cup whole milk

1 cup heavy cream

1 cup grated Parmesan cheese

2 tablespoons crème fraiche or sour cream

2 tablespoons fresh lemon juice

1   Preheat the oven to 450°F. Line a sheet pan with aluminum foil.

2   Place the tenderloin on the sheet pan and very generously salt and pepper the meat on all sides. Roast for 30 to 35 minutes for medium rare. Transfer to a cutting board and let it rest, tented with foil, for about 15 minutes.

3   Meanwhile, make the parsley cream sauce: In a small saucepan, melt the butter over medium heat. Add the shallots, garlic and a sprinkle of salt and simmer for 2 to 3 minutes. (Do not let the shallots and garlic brown.)

4   Transfer the shallot and garlic oil to a blender with the parsley and milk. Reserve the saucepan. Puree on high until you have a smooth green sauce.

5   Meanwhile, pour the cream into the reserved saucepan. Bring to a simmer over low heat. Whisk in the puréed parsley sauce and cook over low heat for about 10 minutes, whisking often to keep it smooth. Add the Parmesan, crème fraiche and lemon juice and whisk until smooth. Season with salt.

6   Thinly slice the beef tenderloin and serve immediately with the parsley cream sauce drizzled on top and extra sauce in a bowl on the side.

Chocolate Raspberry Tart

Out of the many, many desserts I have made over the years, this one may be the most spectacular looking for the least amount of effort. And let's not forgot to mention that the taste is nothing short of divine. It's perfect for a special occasion when you want to show off, without stressing yourself out. Wow everyone, and when they are oohing and ahhing over the luxurious dessert you must have slaved over, your secret will be safe with me.

SERVES 6 TO 8
PREP TIME: 20 MINUTES
COOK TIME: 20 MINUTES

CHOCOLATE SHORTBREAD CRUST

⅔ cup all-purpose flour

⅓ cup dark cocoa powder

½ cup powdered sugar

½ teaspoon salt

½ cup (1 stick) cold unsalted butter, cut into small pieces

CHOCOLATE GANACHE

8 ounces chocolate

¾ cup heavy cream

2 teaspoons vanilla extract

2 tablespoons unsalted butter

pinch of salt

12 ounces fresh raspberries

INGREDIENT NOTE: Instead of raspberries you could easily substitute blackberries, red currants, small strawberries or apricot slices for an equally fabulous dessert.

1 Preheat the oven to 400°F. Prepare a 9 x 3-inch tart pan with baking spray.

2 First make the shortbread crust: In a food processor, combine the flour, cocoa, sugar and salt and pulse to combine. Add the butter and pulse until a moist dough forms. Transfer to the prepared tart pan and press it in evenly and firmly into the pan.

3 Bake for about 12 minutes, then pull the tart shell out out of the oven and poke a few shallow holes in it to release steam. Press the dough down firmly with the back of a spoon or the bottom of a measuring cup. Stick the tart shell back in the oven to bake for another 5 minutes.

4 Remove the tart shell from the oven and stick the shell in the freezer to cool. (Preparing everything else will take about 10 to 15 minutes—enough time to cool the tart shell).

5 Meanwhile, prepare the ganache: Put the chocolate in a heat-proof bowl.

6 In a small pot, whisk together the cream and vanilla and bring to a simmer over low heat. Pour the cream mixture over the chocolate and whisk until smooth. Add the butter and salt and whisk until the ganache is smooth and glossy.

7 Remove the tart shell from the freezer and pour the ganache into the cooled tart shell. Let the tart sit for about 10 minutes while the ganache sets. Then carefully release the tart from the tart pan and place on a serving platter. Line up the raspberries on top of the tart.

8 Slice and serve at room temperature.

Christmas Morning Breakfast

MENU

- HOMEMADE HOT CHOCOLATE

- BLOOD ORANGE MIMOSAS

- SCRAMBLED EGGS WITH CHEDDAR AND CHIVES

- CARAMEL APPLE STICKY BUNS

I am pretty sure that no one is confused about the primary focus of Christmas morning, and it's not the food. But in my house, there are a few rules that we all abide by. One: Please don't get out of bed unless there is a 7 displayed on the clock. Two: Stockings only until after breakfast. Three: Whoever makes it to the kitchen first, please turn Mommy's coffee maker on. After that, all I care about is watching my children enjoy Christmas. That means taking in the sight of the shiny wrapped gifts under the tree, gaping at how Santa and the reindeer ate the snacks they left out and, of course, drinking hot chocolate and eating sticky buns.

Knowing that my husband, (Santa's little helper) was undoubtedly up until all hours of the night yielding screwdrivers and wrenches, I like to make sure I have hot coffee and a celebratory mimosa ready when he sleepily makes it downstairs. After all, anyone who has successfully put together a Barbie Dream House deserves a little celebration.

Homemade Hot Chocolate

My children can't ever seem to get enough hot chocolate in the cold months. I tend to make this in large batches and store it in my pantry so that whenever the craving hits, I have a good-quality mix on hand and we are just minutes from a hot cup of homemade hot chocolate. The hot chocolate mix below is enough for 6 servings.

GENEROUS TIP: You can make homemade hot chocolate even more fantastic, customizing it to your occasion, by adding a wide range of flavors. Some of my favorite mix-ins are crushed peppermints or candy canes; almond, hazelnut or vanilla extract; cayenne pepper; cinnamon; a scoop of peanut butter; some crushed raspberries; or a few white chocolate chips. The possibilities are endless and wonderful!

SERVES 2
PREP TIME: 5 MINUTES
COOK TIME: 5 MINUTES

HOT CHOCOLATE MIX

1 cup powdered sugar

½ cup dark unsweetened cocoa powder

2 cups whole milk

½ cup Hot Chocolate Mix

4 large marshmallows (optional)

1 Mix together the powdered sugar and cocoa powder in a bowl. Store the hot chocolate mix in an airtight container in your pantry for up to 6 months.

2 In a medium pot, bring the milk to a simmer. Add the hot chocolate mix and whisk until well combined.

3 Pour the hot cocoa into mugs and top with marshmallows, if desired.

Blood Orange Mimosas

Here is a slight variation on a very traditional breakfast cocktail: a mimosa. By substituting fresh blood orange juice for regular, you get a slightly more intense flavor and a spectacular color that's fit for any party!

SERVES 2
PREP TIME: 3 MINUTES

4 ounces blood orange juice

8 ounces chilled champagne

Pour the blood orange juice into a chilled champagne flute, and top off with chilled champagne.

Scrambled Eggs with Cheddar and Chives

There is a trick to making the most delicious scrambled eggs that runs a little deeper than just the obvious additions of butter, milk, white cheddar and sour cream (although these certainly help). It is the way that you cook the eggs that makes the biggest difference! Low and slow is the name of the game, and the trick to getting that fluffy, velvety texture.

SERVES 4 TO 6
PREP TIME: 5 MINUTES
COOK TIME: 5 MINUTES

2 tablespoons unsalted butter

10 large eggs

3 tablespoons whole milk

2 tablespoon sour cream, plus more for garnish

1 cup shredded white Cheddar cheese

kosher salt and freshly ground black pepper

2 tablespoons fresh snipped chives, for garnish

1　In a large pan, melt the butter over low heat, making sure that the butter does not start to brown.

2　Meanwhile, in a medium bowl, combine the eggs, milk, sour cream and cheddar cheese. Whisk or fork-whip the egg mixture until very fluffy and well combined. Add the egg mixture to the hot pan, making sure the heat is on low and that the pan has not gotten hot enough to brown the butter. Cook over the lowest of heat, constantly stirring the eggs with a heatproof spatula.

3　Take the eggs off the heat just before they are completely cooked, as there will be some carryover cooking. Season with salt and pepper.

4　Transfer to a platter or plates and garnish with a dollop of sour cream and some chives. Serve immediately.

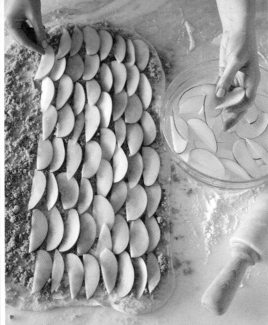

Caramel Apple Sticky Buns

As a child, Christmas morning sticky buns were a once-a-year-treat that we looked forward to almost as much as the gifts under the tree. Now I make Christmas morning sticky buns for my own children. I keep the traditional toasted pecans, but add thin layers of sour apples and dark, gooey caramel. The result lies somewhere between a caramel apple and the sticky buns I grew up with, and they are totally tradition worthy.

MAKES 16 BUNS
PREP TIME: 40 MINUTES
(plus rising time)
COOK TIME: 60 MINUTES

SWEET DOUGH

1½ cups whole milk

½ cup plus
    1½ teaspoons sugar

two ¼-ounce packages
    dry active yeast

1 teaspoon kosher salt

½ cup (1 stick) unsalted
    butter

2 large eggs

5 cups all-purpose flour

FILLING

½ cup {1 stick} unsalted
    butter, melted

2 cups brown sugar

2 sweet apples, peeled
    and very thinly sliced

CARAMEL GOO

1 cup (2 sticks) unsalted
    butter

3 cups brown sugar

1 teaspoon kosher salt

1 cup heavy cream

2 cups chopped pecans,
    lightly toasted

2 tablespoons unsalted
    butter, melted

1   First make the sweet dough: Heat ½ cup of the milk and 1½ teaspoons of the sugar until the sugar has barely dissolved. Transfer to the bowl of a standing mixer and wait until the temperature reads 110°F as measured on a candy thermometer. Add the yeast and let sit for 20 minutes, or until very puffy.

2   Meanwhile, in a saucepan over medium heat, warm the remaining 1 cup milk, the remaining ½ cup sugar, the salt and the butter. When the butter has melted, whisk everything together and remove from the heat to cool.

3   When the milk mixture is room temperature, add it to the yeast, along with the eggs and beat until well combined. While the mixer is running on low, add the flour, a little at a time, until it is all incorporated. Then mix the dough with a dough hook on medium speed until it forms a smooth ball, 2 to 3 minutes.

4   Grease a bowl with cooking spray and place the ball of dough in the bowl. Wrap the top tightly with plastic wrap and place the bowl somewhere warm. Let the dough rise for at least 1 hour, and up to 3 hours.

5   Prepare an 18 x 13-inch sheet pan with baking spray. Set aside.

6   On a lightly floured surface, roll out the dough into a large rectangle, about ¼ inch thick.

7   Layer the filling: Using a pastry brush, spread the melted butter over the surface of the dough rectangle. Sprinkle the dough evenly with the brown sugar, and then lay the thinly sliced apples in a single layer over the dough. Gently roll the dough, sugar and apples up into a log. Set aside to rest.

8   Meanwhile, make the caramel goo: In a saucepan, over low heat, heat the butter, brown sugar, salt and cream until the butter has melted and the sugar has dissolved. Whisk until the caramel is thick, creamy and hot. Pour into the prepared sheet pan and sprinkle with the toasted pecans. Slice the log into 16 even rounds and place them in even rows over the caramel-pecan mixture. Cover with plastic wrap and let rise a second time for at least 30 minutes.

9   Preheat the oven to 350°F.

10 Brush the last 2 tablespoons of melted butter over the top of the buns to keep the dough moist while baking. Bake for 45 minutes. If the tops start to get too brown, tent with tin foil.

11 Let the buns cool for about 10 minutes before flipping upside down onto a platter. Serve immediately or at room temperature.

New Year's Eve Cocktail Party

MENU

- ROASTED TOMATO BASIL SOUP WITH GRILLED CAMBOZOLA AND BACON SANDWICHES

- LOBSTER MACARONI AND CHEESE

- CAULIFLOWER RISOTTO

- MANGO CHUTNEY TARTLETS WITH BBQ DUCK

- CHICKEN AND GUINNESS POT PIE

- CHOCOLATE CARAMEL MOUSSE

- BLOOD ORANGE SORBET

One of the great joys of where our house is situated, on the top of a hill overlooking Seattle, is that we have a lovely view of the city. Every year, on New Year's Eve, the clock strikes twelve and a sparkling fireworks display, launched from the Space Needle, lights up the night sky. This view has encouraged us beyond the usual New Year's festivities when we host friends and family each year. Sometimes we celebrate it is a casual Game Night (see page 140), sometimes a more formal sit-down dinner party (see page 172), and other years, a cocktail party where I serve a selection of appetizers.

This particular menu is a favorite, as it is inspired by my husband. He just loves old-fashioned comfort food like pot pies and macaroni and cheese (don't all men?). I took those dishes and several more and not only elevated them to something more sophisticated, but made them practical to serve in miniature form if you wish. These are guaranteed to be crowd pleasers.

BUBBLY BAR

It's practically a given that you will serve bubbly on New Year's Eve. It's synonymous with celebrations! However, do not assume that you can only serve champagne. There are plenty of other sparkling wines such as prosecco, cava and sweet muscato that are also delicious, and oftentimes less expensive.

When building a Bubbly Bar, I like to serve my sparkling wines very cold and on ice, with a selection of options for building lovely champagne cocktails. My favorites are fresh berries, fruit purees, juices and liquors. If you are doing self serve, set up the mix-ins on a buffet with labels, and provide lots of champagne glasses, cocktail stir sticks and bubbly on ice!

CREATIVE WAYS TO SERVE APPETIZERS

I'm obsessed with unique and quirky ways of presenting food. The small portion size of appetizers make them perfect for playing around with proportions and serving vessels!

• Chinese soup spoons: A very convenient way (with built-in handle) of serving one-bite appetizers without ever dirtying anyone's hands!

• Vintage forks: I collect random forks at vintage and junk stores and use them for appetizers (I actually like that they don't match). They are great for twirling a single mouthful of pasta, or spearing a single shrimp or bite of nectarine with ripe cheese. Again—no dirty hands!

• Demitasse cups: These heatproof vessels are exceptionally versatile. They are wonderful for petite portions of hot soups and drinks. I also use them for baking things like mini pot pies and individual macaroni and cheeses.

• Sake cups: Similar to the demitasse, but smaller and without the handle. These come in a wide variety of inspiring colors and textures.

• Votives: Clear glass votives are perfect for individual portions of dip and crudités, thing like tuna tartare with a crisp, or tomato chutney with a spear of toasted baguette. If they are the taller variety, I also use them for chilled soups like gazpacho.

• Cordial glasses: Varying from 1 to 3 ounces, these are perfect for serving gulps of cold soup or mini smoothies or juices.

Roasted Tomato Basil Soup with Grilled Cambozola and Bacon Sandwiches

This best-ever tomato basil soup gets its great depth of flavor from roasting the tomatoes. And is there anything better to dunk into hot tomato soup than a grilled cheese sandwich? This grown-up version pairs a creamy blue-streaked cheese with salty bacon for the ultimate soup and sandwich combo.

SERVES 4 TO 6 OR 24 MINIS
PREP TIME: 10 MINUTES
COOK TIME: 60 MINUTES

3 pounds tomatoes, preferably on the vine

5 garlic cloves, unpeeled

¼ cup olive oil

kosher salt

2 tablespoons butter

1 large yellow onion, roughly chopped

handful of fresh basil leaves, plus more for garnish

2 quarts chicken stock

½ cup heavy cream

GRILLED CAMBOZOLA AND BACON SANDWICHES

PREP TIME: 10 MINUTES
COOK TIME: 15 MINUTES

8 strips thick-cut bacon

8 ounces Cambozola Cheese

8 thin slices rustic bread

handful of fresh basil leaves

2 tablespoons butter

1 First make the soup. Preheat the oven to 400°F.

2 Arrange the tomatoes and garlic on a sheet pan. Drizzle with the olive oil and sprinkle with salt. Roast for 30 minutes, then set aside to cool.

3 In a soup pot, melt the butter over medium heat. Add the onion and sweat until tender, about 5 minutes. (it is okay if the onion starts to caramelize).

4 Squeeze the roasted garlic from their skins and add the garlic, tomatoes and any juices into the soup pot, along with the basil and chicken stock. Adjust the heat to medium-high and cook for about 15 minutes.

5 Meanwhile, make the sandwiches. Cook the bacon in a medium pan over medium-high heat until all of the fat has been rendered and the bacon is very crispy. Transfer to a paper towel to drain.

6 Divide the Cambozola among 4 bread slices and top each with a few leaves of basil and 2 strips of crispy bacon. Top the fillings with the second piece of bread so you have 4 sandwiches.

7 Heat a griddle or grill pan over medium heat. Add the butter, a few teaspoons for each sandwich, and fry the sandwiches in batches until golden brown on the bottom, about 3 minutes. Flip the sandwiches (adding more butter) and cook until both sides are golden brown and the cheese has melted. Transfer the sandwiches to a cutting board and slice each into 6 small pieces.

8 Remove the soup from the heat. Using an immersion blender, puree the soup until completely smooth. Stir in (do not blend!) the heavy cream. Taste and adjust the seasoning. Garnish with fresh basil leaves.

9 Serve the sandwiches hot alongside the tomato soup.

Lobster Macaroni and Cheese

I must confess: This is another recipe that I borrowed from my husband, who makes a mean macaroni and cheese. But I dressed it up to create an elegant New Year's dish. Not only is this a white cheese sauce, but there is nothing like the addition of fresh lobster and bright green onions to elevate this classic. Serve with green salad for dinner, or bake into miniature serving dishes to create hors d'ouevres.

SERVES 6 TO 8 OR 24 MINIS
PREP TIME: 20 MINUTES
COOK TIME: 60 MINUTES

1 tablespoon butter,
   for greasing dish

1 pound uncooked
   lobster tail

1 pound small pasta shells

1 recipe White Cheese Sauce
   (see below)

½ cup thinly sliced
   green onions

WHITE CHEESE SAUCE

¼ cup unsalted butter

¼ cup all-purpose flour

3 cups whole milk

8 ounces Gruyère, grated

8 ounces Monterey Jack,
   grated

1 garlic clove, minced

¼ teaspoon cayenne pepper

pinch of ground nutmeg

kosher salt and freshly
   ground black pepper

1 Preheat the oven to 350°F. Prepare a 9 x 13 x 2-inch baking dish with the butter. (If using individual serving dishes, just make sure they are ovenproof.) Set a large pot of salted water to boil.

2 Using sharp kitchen shears, cut the raw lobster tail open and gently remove the raw meat. Chop into bite-sized pieces and set aside.

3 Make the white cheese sauce: Melt the butter in a heavy pot over medium heat. Add the flour and, using a whisk, mix the butter and flour together until smooth, then cook for 4 to 6 minutes, or until the sauce is still pale, but the raw flour taste is gone. (This is a roux.)

4 Add the pasta to the boiling water and cook it a few minutes less than al dente, according to package directions.

5 Meanwhile, add the milk to the roux and stir until there are no lumps. Add the Gruyère and Monterey Jack, garlic, cayenne pepper and nutmeg. Stir really well until the sauce is smooth. Season with salt and pepper.

6 Drain the pasta when it's done and add it to the cheese sauce with the green onion and raw lobster pieces. Toss to coat. Transfer to the prepared baking dish or dishes.

7 Bake for about 25 minutes, or until the top is golden and crispy. Serve immediately.

Cauliflower Risotto

This risotto blends snowy white cauliflower with creamy Arborio rice. I really enjoy the additions of the golden raisins and toasted walnuts, as they not only provide sweet and earthy flavors, but a range of textures to the risotto. This could be served not only as an elegant main course at a dinner party, but also as a rustic weeknight meal. When spooned into small soup spoons or egg cups, it also makes a tantalizing hors d'houevre.

GENEROUS TIPS: Truffle oil, while a luxury, lasts a long time stored in a cool dark place. A little goes a long way, and like the Cauliflower Soup on page 14, this Cauliflower Risotto is well suited to a little drizzle on top. Because you are adding simmering chicken stock to the risotto a little at a time, it's best to set the two pots next to each other on the stovetop.

SERVES 4 TO 6 OR 24 MINIS
PREP TIME: 10 MINUTES
COOK TIME: 30 MINUTES

1½ quarts chicken stock

3 tablespoons butter

2 tablespoons olive oil

1 yellow onion, minced

2 cups very small cauliflower florets

1½ cups Arborio rice

1 cup white wine

1 cup finely grated Parmesan, plus more for garnish

kosher salt

¼ cup golden raisins

¼ cup walnut pieces, toasted

fresh herbs, for garnish (whatever is on hand)

truffle oil, for drizzling (optional)

1 In a medium saucepan, bring the chicken stock to a simmer over low heat.

2 Meanwhile, melt the butter and the olive oil together in a large sauté pan. Add the onion and sweat over medium-low heat until tender, about 5 minutes. Add the cauliflower and sweat another 2 minutes. Add the Arborio rice and cook until the rice is translucent on the outside and opaque in the center, about 3 minutes. Add the white wine and, using a wooden spoon, stir and stir, scraping up any bits stuck to the bottom of the pan.

3 Begin to add the simmering chicken stock, a cup at a time, to the risotto, while you just stir and stir. After each cup of stock is cooked into the rice and the risotto begins to dry out, you ladle another cup in. This process usually takes about 20 minutes total, or until the rice is tender.

4 Remove the risotto from the heat. Stir in the Parmesan and then season with kosher salt. Add the raisins and walnuts and stir well.

5 Garnish with extra Parmesan, a sprinkle of herbs and, if desired, a drizzle of truffle oil. Serve hot.

Mango Chutney Tartlets with BBQ Duck

These tartlets, which come from my catering days, feature one of my most unique flavor combinations. A sweet and anise-spiced Mango Chutney pairs superbly with a bite of smoky BBQ duck and a crown of brilliant Caramelized Red Onions. I purchase good-quality premade tartlet shells and BBQ duck breast to save time, and the chutney and onions are even better if they are prepared the day before.

GENEROUS TIP: You will have ½ cup of Mango Chutney left over—it tastes great on roasted pork tenderloin, grilled salmon or with goat cheese on crostini—plus three-quarters of the Caramelized Red Onions, which can be used in quiche, frittata, sandwiches and enchiladas.

MAKE AHEAD: If you make the Mango Chutney and Caramelized Red Onions at least a day ahead, the flavors will develop, and the assembling and baking for this dish will take just 10 minutes.

MAKES 24 TARTLETS
PREP TIME: 20 MINUTES
COOK TIME: 50 MINUTES

MANGO CHUTNEY

1 tablespoon unsalted butter

¼ cup minced yellow onion

1 large mango, peeled, pitted and diced

1 star anise

¼ cup water

2 teaspoons sugar

2 teaspoons red wine vinegar

kosher salt

CARAMELIZED RED ONIONS

1 tablespoon unsalted butter

1 red onion, thinly sliced

kosher salt

1 cup water

1 tablespoon sugar

1 tablespoon red wine vinegar

Twenty-four 2-inch mini tartlet shells

½ cup Mango Chutney

1 breast BBQ duck, cut into bite-sized pieces

¼ cup Caramelized Red Onions

1. First make the mango chutney (preferably a day ahead): In a large sauté pan, melt the butter over medium heat. Add the onion and cook until softened but not browned, 2 to 3 minutes. Add the mango and reduce the heat to low. Add the star anise and water, cover, and cook for 15 minutes.

2. Turn the heat up to medium, add the sugar and the vinegar, and stir well. Cook, uncovered, another 5 minutes, or until the liquid has cooked off. Remove from the heat and season with salt. Dispose of the star anise, transfer to an airtight container and refrigerate until ready to use.

3. Next make the caramelized red onions (preferably a day ahead): Melt the butter in a medium sauté pan over medium heat. Add the onion and sprinkle lightly with salt. Cook for 2 minutes, until the onion begins to soften. Add the water and cook over low heat for 15 minutes, until the onions are very soft and tender and the water has cooked off.

4. Sprinkle the onions with the sugar and vinegar. Cook another 2 to 3 minutes, until the onions are dry. Transfer to an airtight container and refrigerate for up to 5 days, or until ready to use.

5. When ready to assemble the tartlets, preheat the oven to 400°F. Line a sheet pan with parchment paper.

6. Arrange all 24 tart shells on the sheet pan. Into each shell, spoon 1½ teaspoons mango chutney, then top with a piece of BBQ duck and ½ teaspoon caramelized red onion.

7. When all of the tarts have been assembled, bake for 5 minutes. Serve immediately.

Chicken and Guinness Pot Pie

This chicken pot pie has come a long way since I was a kid, while still retaining the nostalgia of childhood. Tender chunks of white chicken, vegetables, and crispy pastry are complemented by a rich and creamy broth that is brimming with Guinness and chicken flavor. Incredible on a cold winter's night or baked in individual servings for a party.

SERVES 4 TO 6 OR 24 MINIS
PREP TIME: 20 MINUTES
COOK TIME: 1 HOUR 20 MINUTES

3 large boneless, skinless chicken breasts

kosher salt and freshly ground black pepper

1 package puff pastry (2 sheets), thawed

¼ cup plus 1 tablespoon unsalted butter

1 yellow onion, diced

1 cup chopped carrots

1 cup chopped celery

1 cup frozen peas

1 cup frozen pearl onions

1 medium potato, peeled and diced

two 11-ounce bottles of Guinness beer

¼ cup all-purpose flour

2 cups chicken stock

⅔ cup heavy cream

1 tablespoon fresh thyme leaves

1 large egg

1 teaspoon water

INGREDIENT NOTE: If you don't have Guinness, use another good dark beer.

1   Preheat the oven to 375°F.

2   Arrange the chicken breasts on a sheet pan and sprinkle generously with salt and pepper. Roast the chicken for about 40 minutes, or until the juices run clear. Remove the chicken from the oven to cool slightly but leave the oven at 375°F. When the chicken is cool enough to handle, remove the skin and bones, then shred the meat into bite-sized pieces. Set the meat aside with any juices that have collected on the pan; discard the skin and bones.

3   Grease a 9 x 13 x 2-inch baking dish with 1 tablespoon of the butter.

4   In a large heavy pot, melt the remaining ¼ cup butter over medium heat. Add the onion, sprinkle with a little salt and cook until the onion is soft. Add the carrots, celery, peas, pearl onions and potato. Sweat for 2 to 3 minutes until the vegetables start to soften. Add the shredded chicken pieces and the Guinness and let the vegetables and beer sweat for about 5 minutes, until everything is hot and tender.

5   Stir in the flour to thicken the sauce. Cook for 3 to 5 minutes, stirring often, to get rid of the raw flour taste. Add the chicken stock, cream and thyme. Stir the filling, cover, and let simmer for about 10 minutes. Season with salt and pepper and then pour the filling into the prepared baking dish.

6   On a lightly floured surface, lay the two puff pastry sheets side by side, overlapping where they meet. Using a rolling pin, roll them together so you have a long rectangle (for the smaller pot pies, just cut the sheets to size for each pie.) Using the puff pastry sheet, make a tent over the filling, simply pinching the puff pastry to the edges of the dish to hold it in place. Cut off any extra overhanging dough.

7   Beat the egg with the 1 teaspoon water. Lightly brush the egg wash over the puff pastry. Slice some steam holes in the top of the pie. Carefully put the pot pie in the oven and bake for 20 minutes, or until the insides are bubbling and the puff pastry is golden brown. Cool slightly before serving.

Chocolate Caramel Mousse

I have been making this mousse for 15 years, and it is still as fantastic today as it was the first time I took a bite. The purity of the ingredients—just good dark chocolate, eggs, sugar and cream—create the most rich and luxurious dessert that you could imagine. The added bonus is the surprising ease with which it comes together. It is a phenomenal make-ahead dessert for parties, since you can make and pipe the mousse into serving dishes the day before, and just garnish them before you serve.

GENEROUS TIPS: Should the chocolate not melt all the way into the hot caramel when you pour it over, place the bowl of chocolate caramel over a small pot of simmering water, and watching it very carefully, stir like crazy until smooth—then immediately remove from heat. The consistency will not be like ganache—remember, there is caramel in there. It will look like chocolate caramel, thick and shiny.
   I love to pipe or spoon this mousse into champagne saucers, or aperitif glasses for serving. Beautiful garnishes for this mousse include fresh berries, edible flowers or even just a dollop of freshly whipped cream.

SERVES 4 TO 6, OR 24 MINIS
PREP TIME: 20 MINUTES
(plus chilling time)
COOK TIME: 15 MINUTES

10 ounces dark, good-quality semi-sweet chocolate

3 large egg yolks

½ cup sugar

3 cups heavy whipping cream

fresh berries, edible flowers or dark chocolate shavings, for garnish (optional)

1   Chop the chocolate (the finer the better) and place the pieces in a heatproof bowl.

2   In the bowl of a standing mixer, whisk the egg yolks until very smooth, pale and fluffy.

3   Heat the sugar in a medium saucepan over low heat until it reaches a deep amber color, 5 to 7 minutes.

4   Meanwhile, heat 1 cup of the cream in a small saucepan over low heat until it simmers.

5   When the sugar has reached its amber color, using a wooden spoon, stir in the hot cream. Keep stirring over low heat, until all of the sugar is melted and the caramel is smooth.

6   With the mixer on medium speed, add one spoon of hot caramel at a time to the egg yolks, and making sure to mix well before adding more. (The goal is to temper the egg yolks without scrambling them.) When you have mixed all of the caramel into the yolks, the mixture will still be hot. Immediately pour the caramel over the chocolate. Let sit for a moment, and then stir until all of the chocolate has melted and the mixture is smooth.

7   In a medium bowl, with an electric mixer, whip the remaining 2 cups cream to soft peaks. Add about ¼ cup of the whipped cream to the chocolate caramel and vigorously whisk until the chocolate caramel thins a bit and gets glossy. Fold in half of the remaining whipped cream, then add the remaining whipped cream and fold until the mousse is smooth and uniform.

8   Spoon or pipe the mousse into bowls or glasses. Chill for at least 30 minutes, or until ready to serve.

9   Garnish with fresh berries, edible flowers or chocolate shavings. Serve chilled.

Blood Orange Sorbet

This sorbet is refreshing, palate cleansing and an absolutely gorgeous burnt orange color. I love to serve it in pretty stemmed glasses, presented on a tray with silver spoons. You do not need an ice cream maker for this recipe—the sorbet mix can go directly into the freezer.

MAKES 1 PINT
PREP TIME: 5 MINUTES
(plus freezing time)
COOK TIME: 5 MINUTES

½ cup water

½ cup sugar

pinch of kosher salt

2 cups blood orange juice

fresh blood orange slices,
    for garnish (optional)

1   In a small saucepan, bring the water, sugar and salt to a simmer, whisking to make sure the sugar and salt dissolve. Cook for 3 minutes more, until slightly thickened.

2   Remove from the heat and whisk in the blood orange juice. Let the mixture cool to room temperature, then transfer to a plastic or metal container and freeze overnight.

3   Scoop and serve.

Index

Acknowledgments

Pia and Coco, my little angels on earth. I love you so much, and am grateful for your never-ending inspiration and enthusiasm for all of Mommy's "projects."

My mom and dad, who have nurtured my creativity for as long as I can remember. Thank you for always believing in me and encouraging me to create as much beauty as I can in the world and to share it with everyone.

Tula, thank you for being the greatest yia-yia and mother-in-law, and for so generously sharing your wonderful recipes with everyone.

Jonny and Natalie, Julie and Eric, Chris, Rachel and George, Heather and Dino, I love you. I am so lucky to have such amazing brothers and sisters. Thanks for always having my back.

Jeannine and Danielle for your deep-seeded support and for fielding so much of my craziness as only great girlfriends can.

Judy and Lilly for holding down the fort, constantly taste-testing and always having smiles on your faces.

Thank you, **Janis**, for believing in me and protecting me.

Thank you, **Leslie, Jim, Lisa, Anne, Jean and especially Anja** for helping me make such a beautiful book. Thank you for "getting me," Anja, and seeing what this book could be.

Pete, the love of my life, the light of my life, thank you for each and every day that I get to spend as your wife. You are the most supportive, loving husband in the world and my very best friend— thank you for holding my hand as I make my dreams come true.